Southern
Thymes
Shared

Southern Thymes Shared

Lara Lyn Carter
and
Doc Lawrence

PELICAN PUBLISHING COMPANY
GRETNA 2014

The word "Pelican" and the depiction of a pelican are
trademarks of Pelican Publishing Company, Inc., and are
registered in the U.S. Patent and Trademark Office.

Library of Congress Cataloging-in-Publication Data

Carter, Lara Lyn.
  Southern thymes shared / by Lara Lyn Carter and Doc Lawrence.
      pages cm
  Includes index.
  ISBN 978-1-4556-1866-8 (hardcover : alkaline paper) — ISBN 978-1-4556-1867-
5 (e-book) 1. Cooking, American—Southern style. 2. Food and wine pairing. 3. Table
setting and decoration. 4. Entertaining. 5. Parties. 6. Holiday cooking. I. Lawrence, Doc.
II. Title. III. Title: Southern times shared.
  TX715.2.S68C3783 2014
  641.5975—dc23
                                                                    2013037719

Printed in China
Published by Pelican Publishing Company, Inc.
1000 Burmaster Street, Gretna, Louisiana 70053

Contents

Preface

My first visit to Monticello, the Virginia home of Thomas Jefferson, became a transcendent experience. It was my first introduction to Southern food and its relationship to wine. Like many writers and culinary commentators I know, I more or less accepted the notion that wines are alien to the South and its people, and we are forever consigned to sweet tea with our deep-fried delights. How terribly wrong I was!

I saw the light, to paraphrase Hank Williams, during my self-guided tour of Mr. Jefferson's wine cellar, kitchen, and dining room. The author of the Declaration of Independence maintained a wine cellar loaded with the most renowned bottles from France, Germany, Spain, and Italy, and his journals confirm that the inventory would have been the envy of today's cellar masters.

Jefferson entertained like no other American in his time, and his suppers, the forerunners of today's wine dinner (where courses are matched with carefully selected wines), were notable for fresh vegetables from his gardens seasoned with hog jowl and wines that blended with the aromas and flavors of the meal—a lush white or red Bordeaux for neighbors or heads of state or a Riesling for the Christmas feast of roast wild turkey. Wines were always on the table, and the glasses were refilled until the last bite.

About a year after my enlightenment at Monticello, I had a conversation with a delightful television chef, Lara Lyn Carter, who, with a great deal of excitement in her voice, told me about her recipes and her cooking heritage—South Georgia mixed with Italian—and that proverbial light bulb started to brighten.

I shared my adventures at Monticello, and we both concluded that a cookbook was needed to fully communicate the ties between our food and drink. Anything she produced, I said, could be paired appropriately with wine. It was, we agreed, our third president, who began America's wine traditions.

And so a cookbook featuring wines of the world paired with original Southern recipes was born. Lara Lyn Carter named it *Southern Thymes Shared,* and I believe to my soul that Thomas Jefferson would want a copy in his kitchen.

Doc Lawrence
Stone Mountain, Georgia

Southern
Thymes
Shared

New Year's Day Traditions

Serves 6

Spicy Fried Chicken
Mustard Greens
Slow-Cooker Black-Eyed Peas
Pecan Wild Rice
Celebration Chocolate Cake

With the new year, many people vow to make changes to their lives and do things differently. My New Year's resolution is to never change the family favorites that we eat on this special day! With this menu, I know that my family will start off the new year happy—and full.

Spicy Fried Chicken

If you don't like spice, stay out of the kitchen!

2 eggs
1 cup whole milk
2 tbsp. hot sauce, or to taste
1½ tsp. salt
1 tsp. pepper
2½ lbs. chicken, in pieces
1½ cups self-rising flour
3 cups vegetable shortening

In a large bowl, beat the eggs; add milk, hot sauce, salt, and pepper. Place chicken in the mixture; let sit for 30 minutes. Put the flour in a large bowl or paper bag. Coat chicken with the flour. Melt the shortening in a large cast-iron skillet over medium-high heat. Reduce heat to medium and fry chicken in batches, being sure not to overcrowd the chicken. Cook, covered, until good and crispy, about 25 minutes depending on the thickness of the pieces. Turn halfway through cooking.

Mustard Greens

This Southern dish is another must on New Year's Day. Greens will bring you green money for the new year, so eat up!

3 lb. Boston butt
10 bunches mustard greens, washed, stems removed
2 tsp. sugar
2 tsp. salt
2 tsp. pepper

Place pork in large pot with enough water to cover meat. Cook over medium heat until meat falls apart, about 3 hours. Shred meat into the water and add greens slowly, letting them wilt. Add the sugar, salt, and pepper, and continue to cook over medium-low heat for 2 hours or until tender. After greens are cooked, taste and add more seasonings as needed. Serve with hot pepper sauce for a real Southern tradition!

Slow-Cooker Black-Eyed Peas

Black-Eyed peas are a year-round part of the Southern dining table, often paired with a bottle of hot sauce. On New Year's Day, eating your peas will bring luck in the new year.

2 cups dried black-eyed peas, soaked overnight in water
1 ham hock
1 tbsp. salt
1 tbsp. pepper

Drain peas and place in a slow cooker with ham, salt, and pepper. Cover with water and cook on low for 6 to 8 hours until tender.

Pecan Wild Rice

What a tasty combination of the nutty flavor of the wild rice and the pecans! This is also delicious stuffed in a bell pepper and topped with a sprinkle of parmesan.

2 tbsp. butter
4 cups cooked long-grain wild rice, not instant
Salt and pepper to taste
1 cup chopped, toasted pecans

Melt butter in a skillet. Add the rice and stir to coat. Add salt and pepper as desired. Mix in pecans and serve.

Celebration Chocolate Cake

Cakes don't have to have elegant designs, but they have to taste wonderful. This cake fits the bill on both counts!

For the Cake:
1/2 cup butter
1/2 cup vegetable oil
1 cup water
2 cups sugar
2 cups flour
3 tbsp. cocoa powder
1 tsp. baking soda
1/2 cup buttermilk
2 extra-large eggs
1 tsp. almond extract

For the Icing:
1/2 cup butter
3 tbsp. cocoa powder
1/3 cup half-and-half
3 1/2 cups confectioners' sugar, sifted
1 tsp. almond extract
1 1/4 cup toasted, chopped pecans

To make the cake, melt butter, oil, and water in a sauce pan. Place sugar, flour, cocoa powder, and baking soda in a mixing bowl, and add butter mixture, blending well. Add buttermilk, eggs, and almond extract, blending well. Pour into a greased 9" x 13" sheet pan and bake at 400 degrees for 25 minutes. Allow cake to cool slightly before frosting, but cake should still be a little warm when frosted.

To make the icing, melt butter, cocoa powder, and half-and-half together in a saucepan. In a mixing bowl, combine the powdered sugar, almond extract, and chocolate mixture, beating well; stir in pecans. Spread over slightly warm cake.

Wine Pairing

Champagne is our most popular celebratory wine, and there's no need to shy away from its use as a primary beverage. Winston Churchill reportedly drank it with every meal. Dom Pierre Pérignon, at the moment he discovered champagne, is said to have exclaimed, "Come quickly, I am drinking the stars!" What a way to begin the year! Bubbly has many counterparts, and if you haven't tasted the sparkling wine from Wolf Mountain Vineyards in Dahlonega, Georgia, you have lots of excitement in store. Another delicious choice is the wonderful sparkling wine Gruet Blanc de Noirs from New Mexico.

For Love of Family and Friends— Valentine's Feast

Serves 6-8

Grilled Lamb with Rosemary
Orzo Salad
Grilled Pound Cake with Raspberry Sauce

Not all valentines come with bows and string. This meal can't be opened or read aloud, but it conveys love none the less. The finale of red raspberry sauce on grilled pound cake is better than any box of chocolates!

Grilled Lamb with Rosemary

Lamb is one of those distinctive dishes that always pleases the palate. Much like a Thanksgiving turkey, it is elegant and makes a statement when presented on a table.

3-4 lb. leg of lamb, deboned and tied
4 tbsp. olive oil
2 tbsp. soy sauce
Juice of 1 lemon
Zest of 1 lemon
3 sprigs fresh rosemary
1 clove garlic, minced

Place lamb in a foil-lined baking dish. Whisk together remaining ingredients and pour over the meat. Cover and marinate in the refrigerator overnight. Remove lamb from marinade and discard the rosemary; reserve the marinade. Grill meat, basting frequently with the marinade, until temperature reaches 145 degrees in the center. Allow lamb to rest 20 minutes before serving.

Orzo Salad

I love pasta salads because you can create so many different combinations. This one is very versatile, and the zesty flavors complement the lamb with some extra brightness. Give this dish a try year round if you want a great dish for luncheons or side dish for summer.

2 cups uncooked orzo
$\frac{1}{3}$ cup olive oil
$\frac{1}{3}$ cup sun-dried tomatoes in oil, drained
Juice of 1 lemon
Zest of 1 lemon
$\frac{1}{2}$ cup fresh basil, packed
1 cup feta cheese

Cook orzo in salted water until al dente. Drain and pour into a large bowl. In a food processor, combine oil, tomatoes, lemon juice, lemon zest, and basil until smooth. Pour mixture over orzo and top with crumbled feta cheese. Serve hot or cold.

Grilled Pound Cake with Raspberry Sauce

This is absolutely the best pound cake you will ever eat, so don't be bashful.

For the Cake:
$1/2$ cup margarine, room temperature
$1/2$ cup vegetable shortening
3 cups sugar
5 large eggs
3 cups all-purpose flour
1 cup buttermilk
$1/2$ tsp. baking soda dissolved in 1 tbsp. boiling water
2 tsp. almond extract
Melted butter, for serving

For the Raspberry Sauce:
$1/2$ pt. raspberries
$1/2$ cup sugar
$1/4$ cup water
1 cup raspberry jam
1 tsp. almond extract

To make the cake, beat margarine, shortening, and sugar until fluffy. Add eggs one at a time, beating well after each addition. Slowly add flour, buttermilk, baking soda mixture, and almond extract; beat for 2 to 3 minutes. Pour batter into a greased Bundt pan and bake at 350 degrees for $1/2$ hours or until a toothpick comes out clean.

To make the sauce, combine all ingredients in a saucepan. Heat until sugar and jam are fully combined; simmer for 5 minutes. Pour into a blender and process until smooth. Chill until ready to serve. Reheat the sauce before serving.

To serve, slice the pound cake in $1/2$" to 2" slices. Brush both sides lightly with melted butter. Grill for 1 to 2 minutes on each side until lightly toasted. Place grilled cake on individual plates and drizzle with raspberry sauce.

Wine Pairing

Like a precious and intimate message in a Valentine's Day card, a bottle of Saint-Amour will bring a smile when it is poured and tasted. One of the most romantic of all wines, the name almost says it all. But, with love in the air, there's magic when this delicious wine from the Beaujolais region of Burgundy is in a crystal glass. The wine is among the most versatile and pairs comfortably with the grilled lamb without overpowering.

Elegant Seafood Dinner

Serves 6-8

Seafood Medley
Citrus Salad
Lime Cake

Your guests will toast you in praise of a delicious dinner when you serve this spectacular seafood meal!

Seafood Medley

I have served this at many dinner parties. It makes a beautiful presentation. Serve it over Basmati rice, and then all you need is a nice salad. This is a rich dish that celebrates the best of the gulf coast.

¾ cup all-purpose flour
¾ cup butter, melted
3 cups half-and-half
1½ tsp. cayenne pepper
2 cups freshly grated sharp cheddar cheese
⅔ cups whole milk
¾ cup sherry
1 lb. fresh lump crabmeat
1 lb. medium shrimp, peeled, deveined, and steamed
1 lb. scallops, steamed for 2 to 3 minutes
2 14-oz. cans artichoke hearts, drained and halved
2 8.5-oz. cans water chestnuts, drained and sliced
1 cup slivered almonds
1¼ cups freshly grated parmesan cheese

Preheat oven to 325 degrees. In a large skillet, add flour to melted butter and stir over low heat for 3 to 4 minutes. Add half-and-half and pepper, stirring continuously until thickened. Add cheddar cheese and stir until melted. Slowly pour in milk and sherry, mixing well. Remove from heat. Grease a deep 9" x 13" casserole dish and layer the crab, shrimp, scallops, artichokes, and water chestnuts in the dish. Pour milk mixture over the top and sprinkle with almonds and parmesan cheese. Bake at 325 degrees for 30 minutes until golden and bubbly.

Citrus Salad

Fresh and full of citrus flavor, this salad is simple yet elegant—a perfect match for seafood.

4 cups spring mix salad greens
1 small red onion, thinly sliced
1 large red grapefruit, sectioned
1 large orange, sectioned, juice reserved
1 tsp. orange zest
2 tsp. Dijon mustard
1 tbsp. honey
3 tbsp. white balsamic vinegar
⅓ cup olive oil

Arrange salad, onion, grapefruit, and orange sections on salad plates. In a small dish, combine reserved orange juice, orange zest, mustard, honey, balsamic vinegar, and olive oil. Drizzle over the salads.

Lime Cake

I have always loved Key lime pies. This is a cake that offers that same twist of lime along with the creamy sweetness of cream cheese frosting. Serve it garnished with a slice of lime or sprig of mint.

For the Cake:
1 cup unsalted butter, room temperature
2¾ cups sugar
6 extra-large eggs, room temperature
3 cups all-purpose flour
¼ tsp. baking powder
¼ tsp. salt
1 cup sour cream
5 tbsp. lime zest

For the Frosting:
1 cup cream cheese
½ cup unsalted butter, room temperature
2 cups confectioners' sugar, sifted
3 tbsp. lime zest

To make the cake, grease a tube cake pan with vegetable shortening and line the bottom with parchment to protect the cake. Cream butter and sugar together; add eggs one at a time and blend well. In a separate bowl, combine flour, baking powder, and salt. Add a third of the dry ingredients to the butter mixture. Add half of the sour cream and mix well; repeat alternating dry ingredients with sour cream until everything is incorporated. Add the lime zest and mix well. Pour batter into prepared pan and bake for 1¼ to 1½ hours, until a toothpick comes out clean. Allow to cool for 15 minutes in the pan, then carefully remove the cake onto cake rack to finish cooling. Remove parchment paper.

To make the frosting, combine all ingredients. Spread on cooled cake.

Wine Pairing

When I think of seafood, memories of the Gulf of Mexico are always present. Here, the wine possibilities are nearly endless. Florida-born Blanc du Bois was created by Lakeridge Winery near Orlando, and the flavor profile resembles white wines from Alsace. Louisiana's acclaimed Pontchartrain Vineyards produces a magnificent expression of Blanc du Bois under its Le Trolley label, which seamlessly blends with the flavors of this dinner. A Chablis Cru from Burgundy was a favorite of Ernest Hemingway, and he kept quite a few bottles on hand for dinner guests in his Key West cellar. Known as Chardonnay in Napa and across America, the styles range from dry and crisp to slightly oaked. For baked or fried fish, a white Burgundy is almost always a bull's-eye.

Girl's Luncheon

Serves 6

Vivian's Chicken Salad
Fruit Salad with Mary's Orange Sauce
Herb Biscuits
Strawberry Lemonade

If you have one really good friend in life, you are a lucky person. I am blessed because I have a group of girlfriends that are true treasures. Each and every one of us is different, yet at the core, we share important values. We draw strength and inspiration from one another.

Vivian's Chicken Salad

This is my friend Vivian's recipe. I love chicken salad, and she makes this for our "girl luncheons". I also request it for birthdays, holidays, and any other time I can talk her into making it for me!

4 large chicken breasts, skin-on and bone-in
2 tsp. Chef Paul Prudhomme's Poultry Magic Seasoning
2 tsp. seasoning salt
1 ¹/₂ cups sour cream
1 ¹/₂ cups mayonnaise
1 ¹/₂ cups sliced almonds
1 cup golden raisins

Season the chicken with the poultry seasoning and seasoning salt. Roast the chicken at 350 degrees for 45 to 50 minutes or until cooked through. Allow the chicken to cool. Remove the bone and skin; cut into bite-size pieces. Combine remaining ingredients together with the chicken, mixing well. Cover and chill overnight.

Fruit Salad with Mary's Orange Sauce

No luncheon is complete without a seasonal fruit salad. My friend Mary shared this recipe with me. It came from her mother, a lovely North Carolina lady. When you try it, you will never serve any other fruit salad again. The sauce also is excellent drizzled over pound cake.

For the Fruit:
2 cups strawberries, washed and halved
1¹/₂ cups blueberries, washed
2 cups watermelon or cantaloupe balls
1¹/₂ cups green grapes, washed and halved

For the Orange Sauce:
1 cup sugar
2 tbsp. cornstarch
¹/₄ tsp. salt
³/₄ cup water
1 cup orange juice
¹/₄ cup freshly squeezed lemon juice
¹/₂ tsp. grated orange peel
¹/₂ tsp. grated lemon peel

Combine all fruits together in a large bowl.

To make the sauce, mix the sugar, cornstarch, salt, water, and juices together. Cook over low heat, stirring constantly, until sugar dissolves and sauce thickens. Add grated peels, remove from heat, and chill. Once cool, drizzle over fruit and serve.

Herb Biscuits

These biscuits are so flavorful, you don't need any butter or jam!

2 cups all-purpose flour
1 tsp. salt
1 tsp. baking soda
1 tsp. baking powder
1 cup butter, melted
1 cup sour cream
1½ tbsp. herbes de Provence

Mix all ingredients together. Bake in mini-muffin tins at 400 degrees for 10 to 12 minutes or until golden brown.

Strawberry Lemonade

Nothing is more refreshing than lemonade on a summer day. This is a recipe that is easy to change up with another berry if strawberries aren't your favorite.

1 pt. fresh strawberries, washed and stems removed
1 6-oz. can lemonade concentrate
1 cup sugar, dissolved in 6 cups hot water, cooled

Purée strawberries in a blender with lemonade concentrate. Pour into a pitcher with sugar mixture. Stir well and serve over ice. Garnish with mint.

Easter Dinner

Serves 8-10

Glazed Ham
Three-Cheese Mac 'n' Cheese
Spring Peas with Pancetta and
Caramelized Onions
Dinner Rolls
Honey Butter
Coconut Cake

The traditional Easter egg hunt, beautiful lilies, and the celebration of the Risen Lord . . . gather around the table and share this meaningful day with those you love.

Glazed Ham

This warm and spicy glaze is a surprising spin on a traditional ham glaze. You will receive rave reviews from your guests. If you cannot find mayhaw jelly, substitute with grape, apple, or peach. Any leftovers of this dish make for great ham biscuits the next morning!

12 lbs. smoked ham
1½ cups mayhaw jelly
1 cup brown sugar
1 tsp. dry mustard
2½ tbsp. apple cider vinegar
1 tbsp. Worcestershire sauce
¾ tsp. ground ginger

Place ham on a baking sheet and cover with foil. Bake at 375 degrees. While ham cooks, make the glaze by combining the remaining ingredients in a saucepan. Cook over low heat until melted; stir well. After the ham has cooked for 30 minutes, remove ham from the oven and baste with the glaze; repeat process twice. Allow ham to stand for 20 minutes before slicing.

Three-Cheese Mac 'n' Cheese

No one who tried this would say that macaroni and cheese is just for kids.

1 lb. elbow macaroni
$^1/_2$ cup butter, melted
2 cups shredded sharp cheddar cheese
2 cups cubed Velveeta cheese
1 tsp. cayenne pepper
2 eggs, beaten
$^3/_4$ cup cream
1 tsp. salt
$^3/_4$ cup parmesan cheese

Cook macaroni in boiling water until al dente. Drain. Pour noodles into a large bowl and add butter. Add the cheddar, Velveeta, and cayenne pepper to the macaroni and stir well. In a separate dish, whisk eggs, cream, and salt together. Pour egg mixture over the macaroni mixture, stirring well. Pour mixture into a greased 9" x 13" baking dish. Sprinkle top with parmesan. Cover dish with foil and bake at 350 degrees for 30 minutes. Uncover and bake an additional 10 minutes until lightly browned.

Spring Peas with Pancetta and Caramelized Onions

Fresh English peas are only available for a few short weeks every year, so enjoy them while they last! This is a dish you won't want to miss.

4 cups fresh English peas
2 tsp. salt, plus additional to taste
¾ cup diced pancetta
1 tbsp. butter
2 medium Vidalia onions, thinly sliced
1 tsp. sugar
Pepper to taste

Cover peas with water; add salt. Bring peas to a boil, cover, and reduce heat to low for 45 to 50 minutes or until tender. While peas cook, brown pancetta in a skillet over medium heat. Remove pancetta from skillet and drain on paper towels. Melt butter in the same skillet; add onion and sugar and sauté until onions soften and begin to caramelize. When peas are done, drain and pour into a serving bowl. Mix in the pancetta and onions and add salt and pepper to taste. Serve warm.

Dinner Rolls

Nothing warms the heart like the smell of fresh baked bread.

2 ¼-oz. packages active dry yeast
½ cup sugar
2 cups warm water
⅔ cups vegetable oil
5 cups self-rising flour

In a large mixing bowl, dissolve the yeast in sugar and water. Let sit for 5 minutes. Add the oil. Slowly add the flour, one cup at a time, mixing well after each cup. Cover dough with a damp cloth and place in the refrigerator. At this point, raw dough will keep for several days, if needed. Roll out dough and place in a greased bowl. Allow to double in size in a warm area. Coat a 9" x 13" pan with non-stick cooking spray. Separate dough into golf ball-size rolls and place in the pan. Bake at 400 degrees until golden brown, about 10 to 12 minutes.

Honey Butter

Using flavored butters is a simple way to add a nice something extra to a meal.

⅔ cup unsalted butter, room temperature
4 tbsp. honey

Whip both ingredients together. To serve, place on individual butter pats and chill until ready to serve or place whipped butter in a serving dish.

Coconut Cake

This cake makes a wonderfully impressive dessert for any occasion. At Easter, it makes a beautiful centerpiece for a plentiful table.

For the Cake:
2½ cups cake flour, sifted before measuring
2½ tsp. baking powder
1 tsp. salt
1⅔ cups sugar
½ cup butter, room temperature
2 egg yolks
1 tsp. vanilla extract
1 cup whole milk

For the Icing:
2 cups plus 2 tbsp. sugar
1 cup water
½ cup egg whites (about 3 egg whites)
Pinch salt
1 tsp. vanilla
2 cups sweetened coconut

To make the cake, sift dry ingredients together (through sugar) into a large mixing bowl. In a separate bowl, cream the butter, and add egg yolks and vanilla. Add the dry ingredients to the butter mixture, alternating with the milk, beating well after each addition. Beat for 1 minute after all ingredients are combined. Pour batter into 2 greased 9" cake pans, and bake at 350 degrees for 20 minutes. Allow the cake to cool for 5 minutes, then turn onto a rack to finish cooling. Cool completely before frosting.

To make the icing, combine 2 cups of sugar with the water in a saucepan over high heat, stirring constantly until sugar dissolves. When mixture reaches the boiling point, stop stirring. Remove pot from heat. In a large mixing bowl, beat

egg whites, remaining 2 tbsp. sugar, and salt until stiff, and gradually pour in hot sugar mixture, beating constantly. Add the vanilla while still beating. Frost each cake layer with icing; sprinkle generously with coconut. After building the cake layers, frost the outside of the cake and sprinkle with remaining coconut.

Wine Pairing

Châteauneuf-du-Pape is more than just a historic town in the southern Rhone Valley of France. Thanks to wine-loving popes, it is also famous for its full-bodied, spicy red wines. American counterparts are available for this enticing menu. One of many excellent choices is Donelan Cuvée Moriah, a California Syrah that draws inspiration from the great Rhone Valley wine traditions. It is festive yet reverent. A white wine ensures variety, and everyone loves choices. Offer a bottle of wonderful Albariño, the bright and zesty white wine from Galicia in Spain. Serve these wines in lovely crystal stemware and the meaningful feast will become a memorable celebration.

Old-Fashioned Fish Fry

Serves 8

Fried Catfish
Cheese Grits
Mimi's Fig Pickles
Jack Daniel's Peachy Rice Pudding

Fish fries are a Southern tradition, and this menu will have you hook, line, and sinker!

Fried Catfish

I can't remember a summer that didn't have a weekly fish fry on the agenda. Many times we would fish all day, and by late afternoon we would be cooking the delicate fillets to serve alongside traditional favorites. When it comes to frying, never underestimate the value of a paper sack!

1 cup yellow cornmeal
2/3 cup all-purpose flour
1½ tbsp. lemon pepper
4 eggs
2 cups milk
Juice of 1 lemon
20 whole catfish or 30 catfish fillets
Salt and pepper to taste
Oil for frying

In a large paper sack, combine the cornmeal, flour, and lemon pepper. In a shallow baking dish, whisk the eggs, milk, and lemon juice together. Arrange catfish on a large baking sheet and sprinkle with salt and pepper. Soak the fish in egg mixture for 10 minutes, then toss in the paper sack with the dry ingredients. Heat oil in skillet or fryer to 375 degrees, and fry the fish until golden brown on both sides. Drain fish well on paper towels.

Cheese Grits

You can't have a fish fry without cheese grits!

4 cups chicken broth
4 cups water
2 tsp. salt
¼ cup butter
2 cups grits, not instant
3 cups shredded sharp cheddar cheese
1 cup sour cream

Bring broth, water, salt, and butter to a boil. Add grits. Reduce heat to low and simmer for 45 to 60 minutes until tender. Stir in the cheese and sour cream until blended.

Mimi's Fig Pickles

When I give these as a gift or serve them to a new audience, people just go crazy! They may sound unusual, but give them a try. These are delicious with fried chicken, too!

7 lbs. ripe but firm figs
6 cups sugar
2 cups apple cider vinegar
1 tsp. whole cloves
1 tsp. whole allspice

In a large stock pot, cover figs with water. Boil for 20 minutes. Drain the figs and leave in the pot. In a separate pot, bring the sugar, vinegar, cloves, and allspice to a boil; boil until it reaches a syrup state. Pour syrup over figs and simmer for 10 minutes. Place figs and syrup in 4 32-oz. wide-mouth hot jars and seal. Turn jars upside down for 5 minutes before returning them right side up to cool.

Jack Daniel's Peachy Rice Pudding

What do you get when a gentleman named Jack meets a sweet Georgia peach? This dish says it all.

2 dried peaches
4 tbsp. of Jack Daniel's Tennessee Whiskey, divided
1 lemon
⅓ cup medium-grain rice
3 cups whole milk
4 tbsp. sugar
8 tbsp. peach preserves

Chop the peaches into bite-size pieces and place in a bowl. Pour 1 tbsp. Jack Daniel's over the peaches. Using a vegetable peeler, remove the rind from the lemon. Place the lemon rind, rice, milk, and sugar in a pot and bring to a boil; reduce heat and simmer for 15 minutes, stirring often to prevent the mixture from sticking. Drain the residual Jack Daniels from the chopped peaches and stir the peaches into the rice mixture. Remove pudding from the heat and divide evenly into 8 serving bowls. Combine the preserves and remaining 3 tbsp. Jack Daniel's in a saucepan. Heat the mixture over medium-high heat until bubbly. Let the mixture reduce slightly into a glaze. Remove the glaze from the heat and allow to thicken by cooling for a few minutes. Pour the glaze evenly over the pudding, and serve.

Wine Pairing

The fish fry is vintage Deep South, a festive celebration that takes on new meaning when palate-pleasing Chenin Blanc is served. This white delight is widely available as Vouvray from the Loire Valley of France. Be sure to serve chilled! Many wonderful brands are available. Fall Creek Vineyards, Ed and Susan Auler's heralded Texas winery, produces highly regarded Chenin Blanc that incorporates subtle citrus characteristics with a floral and mineral fragrance. These magically combine to give Lara Lyn's recipe a taste partner that will earn rave reviews at the dinner table.

Gulf Coast Fiesta

Serves 6-8

Shrimp Tacos with Spicy Slaw
Black Beans Olé
Fiesta Rice
Peach Salsa
Lemon Pound Cake

You don't have to travel to Mexico to have a fiesta! The Southern twist on this party will have you and your guests celebrating in style.

Shrimp Tacos with Spicy Slaw

I love spending time on the coast and going to the local fish market to get fresh seafood straight from the gulf. This is a favorite to make at the beach.

6 lbs. medium shrimp, peeled and deveined
2 tbsp. olive oil
2 tsp. salt
1 cup mayonnaise
1 tbsp. minced garlic
½ cup chopped scallions
2 tbsp. Creole mustard
1 tbsp. lemon zest
1 tsp. lemon juice
1 16-oz. bag coleslaw mix
8 small soft flour tortillas

Toss shrimp with olive oil and salt and place on a baking sheet. Roast at 400 degrees for 8-10 minutes until cooked through. In a bowl, combine mayonnaise, garlic, scallions, mustard, lemon zest, and lemon juice. Pour over slaw and toss to combine. Warm tortillas and fill with shrimp and slaw mixture. Serve with hot sauce for an extra kick!

Black Beans Olé

These are great as a side. Try them rolled into a tortilla for a vegetarian burrito, too!

1 tbsp. olive oil
1 clove garlic, minced
2 15-oz. cans black beans, rinsed and drained
2 tbsp. water
½ cup chopped scallions
¼ cup chopped cilantro

Heat oil in skillet and sauté garlic for 2 minutes until it becomes fragrant. Add beans and water to the skillet and cover. Simmer on low for 7 to 8 minutes until heated through. Remove skillet from heat and toss in scallions and cilantro. Stir well and serve.

Fiesta Yellow Rice

Fluffy and fragrant, this rice is a party all on its own!

2 tbsp. butter
2 tsp. saffron
2 cups long-grain rice
3¼ cups water
1 tsp. salt

Combine all ingredients together in a pot and bring to a rolling boil. Reduce to low, cover, and cook for 20 minutes until rice is tender and fluffy.

Peach Salsa

You will flip over this Georgia twist on salsa!

1 small red onion, minced
2 large peaches, peeled, pitted, and diced
$\frac{1}{2}$ tsp. sugar
1 tbsp. freshly squeezed lime juice
$1\frac{1}{2}$ tbsp. olive oil
2 tbsp. chopped cilantro
$\frac{1}{2}$ tsp. coarse salt

Place onion and peaches in a bowl. Sprinkle with sugar. Add remaining ingredients and let rest for 20 to 30 minutes so the flavors blend.

Lemon Pound Cake

Lemon always pairs beautifully with fish, and this cake brings a sweet ending that complements the main meal. Simple to prepare, it is also wonderful with coffee the next morning, if there are any leftovers!

1 cup butter, softened
3 cups sugar
$\frac{1}{2}$ cup canola oil
5 eggs, room temperature
Juice and zest of 1 lemon
$\frac{1}{2}$ tsp. salt
$3\frac{2}{3}$ cups all-purpose flour
1 cup whole milk

Cream butter. Add sugar, oil, and eggs one at a time. Add lemon juice and zest and salt. Slowly mix in flour and milk until blended well. Pour into a greased Bundt pan, and bake at 350 degrees for 80 minutes.

Wine Pairing

The world of wine has the ongoing promise of new adventures. Vinho Verde has carved out a foothold in America among those who enjoy refreshing white wines. This summertime joy from Portugal reflects the boundless glory of the grape to work magic at the dinner table. It is feather light, flavorful, and quite affordable. Similarly, Muscadet, a soft white wine from the Loire River region of France makes an excellent choice.

Gourmet Cookout

Serves 6

Stuffed Burgers
Grilled Portobello Mushrooms with
Herb Dipping Sauce
Grilled Peaches with Pecans and Cream
Southern Sangria

Don't shy away from a cookout with a menu that impresses, and this one takes the spotlight!

Stuffed Burgers

This is a grown-up hamburger!

1 tbsp. olive oil
1 Vidalia onion, diced
1 tsp. coarse salt
$\frac{1}{2}$ tsp. freshly ground black pepper
2 tsp. sugar
2 lbs. ground round
$\frac{3}{4}$ cup smoked cheddar cheese, cubed
6 Ciabbatta buns, or any bakery-style bun of your choice

Place olive oil in a skillet. Add the onion, salt, pepper, and sugar to the skillet and sauté until tender. Remove onions from skillet and let cool slightly. In a large bowl, combine onions and the beef. Divide beef mixture into 6 equal portions.

Form the beef into balls. Using your finger, make a "canyon" in the middle. Insert the cheese in the groove and mold the beef around the cheese, being sure to cover cheese entirely; shape into a patty without overworking the beef. Grill burgers to desired doneness. Serve on buns.

Grilled Portobello Mushrooms with Herb Dipping Sauce

These mushrooms are so tasty, I could place one on a bun as a burger and never miss the beef.

For the Mushrooms:
6 large Portobello mushrooms, cleaned, stems removed
3 tbsp. olive oil
1 tsp. coarse salt
$^1/_2$ tsp. pepper

For the Herb Sauce:
$^1/_2$ cup mayonnaise
$^1/_2$ cup sour cream
1 tsp. rosemary
1 tbsp. chopped fresh basil
Pinch of salt and pepper
1 clove garlic, minced
Juice of 1 lemon

Brush mushrooms generously with olive oil and sprinkle with salt and pepper. Grill over medium heat until tender, approximately 6 minutes per side.

   To make the herb sauce, combine all ingredients. Serve with mushrooms.

Grilled Peaches with Pecans and Cream

Nothing says Georgia summer like peaches. We use peaches in everything, from cobblers and pies to salsas and salads. This recipe spins a classic dish by using a grill.

6 ripe peaches
Canola oil
3 tbsp. brown sugar
1 tsp. cinnamon
$\frac{1}{4}$ cup toasted pecans
Whipped Cream, for serving
Mint, for garnish

Cut peaches in half and remove pit. Brush lightly with oil and grill 2 to 3 minutes per side, until warm and tender. Remove peaches from grill and slice. In a small bowl, mix together brown sugar, cinnamon, and pecans. Place sliced peaches in a parfait dish, top with a dollop of cream, and sprinkle with cinnamon-sugar mixture.

Southern Sangria

$\frac{1}{4}$ cup sugar
$\frac{1}{4}$ cup warm water
2 oranges
2 lemons
2 750 ml bottles Muscadine wine
$\frac{1}{2}$ cup vodka
1 liter lemon-lime soda

Dissolve the sugar in the warm water. Slice the oranges and lemons into $\frac{1}{4}$" thick slices. Combine all ingredients in a large pitcher and chill well before serving.

Wine Pairing

Summer is sangria time, and few wines are better suited for this than Muscadine. This ubiquitous beverage is wonderful when it's made with this American grape. Close to Lara Lyn's hometown is Still Pond Vineyard, one of the country's top Muscadine producers. Another outstanding group of Muscadine wines comes from Cynthia Connolly's Monticello Vineyards and Winery in North Florida near the Georgia border; their Muscadine is organic, too! While Muscadine is available from sweet to bone dry, use a sweet style as the base wine in a Sangria recipe. Sangria variations are limitless, making this a beverage you can fashion to suit your taste. Poured and served over ice, your Muscadine sangria will refresh your palate and lift your spirits.

Southern Gentleman's Steak Dinner

Serves 6

Whiskey-Marinated Steak Kabobs
Grilled Corn with Herb Butter
Marinated Tomato Salad
Caramel Cake

I have the best group of friends that I could ever ask for. They are sweet, fun, and supportive—everything you could want. We have some of the best times together and laugh a lot. One couple that has been friends of ours for a number of years owns Thirteenth Colony Distillery. How fun is that?

The idea for the distillery arose from a desire to give really unique gifts to friends. I don't think you can get any more unique than spirits, as the motto reads, "made by friends for friends." Thirteenth Colony is located in Americus, Georgia, and was the first legal distillery in the state. They produce bourbon, vodka, gin, corn whiskey, and—their newest product and most fun to cook with—rye whiskey!

As my friend Alton would say, "let me share something with you," and share I will. I have had a ball experimenting with all kinds of recipes using spirits that they have shared with me. The Whiskey Steak Marinade is one of my favorites!

Whiskey-Marinated Steak Kabobs

This marinade, a perfect balance of spice and tang, will become your favorite! Marinate any meat with this recipe for at least 2 hours or overnight.

For the Whiskey Steak Marinade:
2 cloves garlic, minced
1 sweet onion, diced
¼ cup dark brown sugar
¼ cup Worcestershire sauce
¼ cup soy sauce
¼ cup ketchup
2 tbsp. Dijon mustard
Freshly ground black pepper to taste
¼ cup Thirteenth Colony Southern Rye Whiskey
3 sprigs fresh rosemary

For the Kabobs:
6 8-oz. filet mignon steaks
1 Vidalia onion
2 green bell peppers

To make the marinade, mix all ingredients together.

Place steaks in a shallow baking dish. Pour marinade over the steaks, cover, and marinate for 6 to 8 hours. Remove steaks and discard marinade. Cut the steaks into 1½" medallions. Cut onion and peppers in large chunks. Arrange the steak, onion, and peppers on skewers, alternating between each ingredient. Grill over hot coals until desired doneness.

Grilled Corn with Herb Butter

Corn like this not a plain side dish at all. The flavor that comes from the rosemary makes the corn take center stage.

⅓ cup unsalted butter
2 sprigs fresh rosemary
6 ears fresh corn (preferably Silver Queen, if available)
1 tsp. salt
1 tsp. freshly ground black pepper

In a sauté pan, melt butter over medium heat and add rosemary sprigs. Allow the rosemary to infuse the butter for about 10 minutes. Remove pan from heat and discard rosemary. Remove husks and silk from corn and wash. Pat corn dry. Place corn on individual pieces of foil, and brush generously with rosemary butter. Sprinkle with salt and pepper. Wrap up each ear in the foil and place on the grill. Grill corn until tender, approximately 20 minutes, depending on heat.

Marinated Tomato Salad

This tomato salad is as bright as a summer day with its red, yellow, and green colors.

3 ripe red tomatoes
2 yellow heirloom tomatoes
1 cup olive oil
4 tbsp. white balsamic vinegar
3 tbsp. honey
$^1/_2$ tsp. salt
$^1/_2$ tsp. pepper
$^1/_4$ cup chopped fresh parsley
$^1/_4$ cup chopped fresh basil

Cut tomatoes into 6 wedges each and place in a bowl. In a separate dish, whisk all other ingredients together; pour over tomatoes. Stir to coat the tomatoes well, and chill. Allow to marinate for at least 1 hour before serving.

Caramel Cake

Caramel cake is a popular cake. Like someone's favorite candy bar, people are very particular about their caramel cakes! This one comes from my husband's grandmother and is sure to be well loved in your home. I recommend using a candy thermometer when preparing the icing.

For the Cake:
1 cup vegetable shortening
2 cups sugar
4 eggs
2 tsp. vanilla
3 cups all-purpose flour
1 tsp. baking soda
$^3/_4$ tsp. salt
1 cup buttermilk

For the Icing:
4 cups sugar, divided
1²/₃ cups milk
2 tbsp. light corn syrup
¹/₂ cup butter
Pinch salt

Cream shortening and sugar together. Add the eggs, one at a time, and beat after each addition. Add the vanilla. In a separate bowl, whisk together flour, baking soda, and salt. Alternate adding the dry ingredients with the buttermilk to the sugar mixture. Bake in 3 8" round greased and floured cake pans at 325 degrees until cake is golden and a toothpick comes out clean. Allow to sit for 5 minutes before turning onto a rack to cool before icing.

To make the icing, melt 1 cup sugar in a heavy saucepan while stirring constantly until sugar becomes syrup. In a separate saucepan at the same time, cook the remaining 3 cups sugar, milk, and corn syrup. Bring this mixture to a rolling boil, then add the sugar syrup. Cook mixture to the soft-ball stage. Place butter and salt in a mixing bowl and pour hot sugar mixture over the butter. Beat icing until cool enough to spread on cake layers.

To build the cake, alternate cake layers with a layer of icing. Once constructed, cover top and sides of cake with remaining icing.

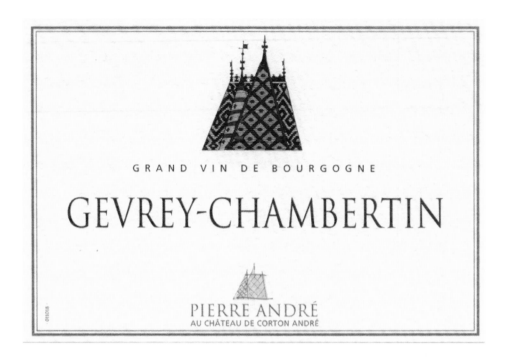

GRAND VIN DE BOURGOGNE

GEVREY-CHAMBERTIN

PIERRE ANDRÉ
AU CHÂTEAU DE CORTON ANDRÉ

Wine Pairing

This meal would inspire a smile from Thomas Jefferson. Not only was he a founding father of America but also he was our first important wine promoter. Favoring French wines and dedicated to entertaining at Monticello, where vegetables grown in his revolutionary garden were always served. Today, a great Pinot Noir such as Gevrey-Chambertin pays homage to our Deep South tradition of hospitality. Versatility is a hallmark of this delicious red Burgundy, which was also one of Napoleon's favorites. Just imagine if he had escaped exile and lived out his days in the French Quarter of New Orleans—this wonderful wine might have become the most popular in Dixie. This classic Pinot Noir is a Burgundy at its best, a red wine for the ages.

Firecracker Barbecue

Serves 8

Slow-Cooker Boston Butt
Whiskey Sauce
Red Potato Salad
Peach Ice Cream

With peach ice cream served straight from the churn and classic barbecue dishes, you are sure to sparkle like fireworks at your own Independence Day celebration.

Slow-Cooker Boston Butt

This is the easiest way to cook up some full-flavor barbecue. The pork is so tender that you can shred it with a fork.

1 tbsp. smoked paprika
1 tbsp. garlic powder
2 tbsp. brown sugar
1 tbsp. seasoned salt
5 lb. Boston butt

In a small bowl, combine all seasonings. Rub mixture onto meat. Put pork in a slow cooker; cook on high for 4 hours, then reduce to low setting for 4 more hours until it falls apart. Serve with Whiskey Sauce.

Whiskey Sauce

This is the perfect combination of sweet and tangy, with a little warmth from the whiskey. This sauce is great with chicken, too.

3 tbsp. canola oil
1 Vidalia onion, minced
2 cloves garlic, minced
1 cup ketchup
1 cup tomato sauce
½ cup brown sugar
½ cup apple cider vinegar
1 tbsp. Worcestershire sauce
2 tbsp. dry mustard
2 tbsp. lemon juice
3 tbsp. rye whiskey

Heat oil in a skillet over medium heat. Sauté the onion and garlic together until tender. Add remaining ingredients and reduce heat to low. Simmer for 30 minutes, stirring frequently. Serve warm or cold.

Red Potato Salad

No cookout is complete without potato salad. I love the buttery flavor red potatoes give this crowd pleaser. This is delicious served either warm or cold.

5 cups diced red potatoes
1 cup chopped scallions
¾ cup mayonnaise
¾ cup sour cream
2 tbsp. red wine vinegar
10 slices bacon, cooked and crumbled
¼ cup chopped fresh parsley
1 tsp. salt
Freshly ground black pepper to taste

Place potatoes in a large pot and add enough water to cover. Cook for 15 to 20 minutes until tender but not mushy. Drain potatoes and transfer to a large bowl. In a separate dish, mix together all remaining ingredients; pour over potatoes. Toss potatoes to coat.

Peach Ice Cream

Summer goodness, here we come!

4 cups peeled and chopped fresh peaches
1 cup sugar
1 3.75-oz. package French vanilla pudding
2 tsp. vanilla extract
1¼ cups cream
1 14-oz. can sweetened condensed milk
2 cups half-and-half
2 cups whole milk

In a large bowl, combine the peaches and sugar. Allow mixture to sit for 1 hour. Using a potato masher, mash the peaches to break up slightly. Do not over-mash the peaches. Pour remaining ingredients over peach mixture, stirring until mixed well. Pour mixture into an ice cream machine and freeze according to machine directions.

Wine Pairing

Barbecue is great with the proper wine, and there are many more choices than often imagined, including a Cru Beaujolais from France such as Moulin à Vent or another delicious red such as Chambourcin from any number of Southern wineries. A sparkling wine will add to the barbecue experience by adding the subtle, refreshing taste of natural fruit. A Cava from Spain, a highly affordable bubbly, takes well to good barbecue, as does Prosecco. The secret to pairing a wine with barbecue is that it should taste wonderful, be served chilled, and not be overwhelmed by fat and spices. With these wines, dinner guests will be surprised and elated.

You're Invited to Sunday Supper

Serves 8-10

Fried Herb Chicken
Creamed Corn
Cornbread
Cornbread Salad
Peanut Butter Pie
Mint Sweet Tea

Like any Southern lady, I know that when someone has family visiting from out of town, you bring food to welcome them. Well, when the family is coming from London, England, there can be a little pressure to make sure that the food you take is not only delicious but really says "Welcome"! When my friends John and Caron O'Hanlon, originally from England, invited my family and me over for Sunday supper to meet his visiting parents, I decided to take over a couple of things that I thought they would enjoy. Number one on my list was my cornbread salad recipe. With ingredients such as cornbread, Vidalia onions, and, of course, fresh Georgia summer tomatoes, how could I go wrong? Not only is the recipe always a crowd pleaser, but it also travels well and goes with just about anything.

This particular menu was inspired by a Sunday school picnic. Our Sunday School class decided to hold an old-fashioned outdoor picnic, similar to ones from days gone by, complete with fried chicken, baked ham, potato salad, cornbread, and other Southern "fine foods." It was to be a great Saturday afternoon at the church's campgrounds. The day was filled with games for the kids, fishing in the pond, socializing for the adults, and, of course, a pie contest, in which the entrants later served their creations as desserts.

The class invited Dr. Kea, the preacher, to be the judge of the contest. I looked as he walked down the table, which was laden with a plethora of beautiful pies of every kind imaginable: fruit pies, custard pies, pies with meringues, and my "Perfect Creation," which had received rave reviews from family and friends. He took a small bite of each pie, smiling after each taste, and moved on to the next. Finally, he reached my pie. I watched him take a bite and waited for his eyes to roll as if he had just tasted the best thing that he had ever put in his mouth. Yes, I got an eye roll—but not one of joy! He looked as though I had filled the pie with dirt! He regained his composure, took a sip of water and moved on to the next pie.

Heartbroken, I waited patiently for him to complete the judging and pick a winner. I cannot even remember which pie won. All I knew was that I had to confiscate my pie before anyone else could taste it to find out what had gone wrong. The exact second the contest was over, I tried to make my way to the pie before anyone else could get a piece. I was mortified by the thought that everyone would be having the same eye-roll reaction to my pie. But the table was rushed by people eager to pick their dessert, and when I did reach the table, my pie was gone. *Oh no*, I thought, I was surely to be the talk of the day. To my relief, people came up to me to say how wonderful the peanut butter pie tasted. What a relief! But now, I was as perplexed as ever to Dr. Kea's reaction. Later that day, Mary Dale, the preacher's wife, came up to me and told me how delicious the pie tasted! I had to ask: "Mary Dale, why do you think Dr. Kea made such a face when he tasted my pie?" Her response? "Honey, he hates peanut butter!" I was ecstatic. I *had* created a wonderful pie! The moral of this story: before serving my Peanut Butter Pie, make sure that your guests are peanut-butter lovers.

Fried Herb Chicken

Nothing is more traditional than fried chicken at Sunday supper in the South. When you add fresh herbs, it puts a new twist on a classic. The herbs bring fresh flavor to the chicken and create the perfect main dish for your table. I like to roughly chop them to help release their flavor. Don't chop them too finely, though.

2 cups buttermilk
2 cups whole milk
3 long sprigs rosemary
5 sprigs thyme
3 tbsp. salt, divided
Juice of 2 lemons
2 whole chickens, cut in pieces
1 lb. all-purpose flour
1 tbsp. pepper
Oil, for frying

In a small bowl, combine buttermilk, whole milk, rosemary, thyme, 1½ tbsp. salt, and lemon juice. Lay chicken in shallow baking dish, and pour milk mixture over chicken. Allow to marinate for at least 2 hours, turning every 30 minutes. Mix together flour, remaining 1½ tbsp. salt, and pepper, and pour into a large, brown grocery bag. Remove chicken from marinade and drain slightly. Place chicken in bag and shake bag to coat. Place two inches of oil in a cast-iron skillet or frying pan over medium heat. Fry chicken, a few pieces at a time, for about 20 minutes. Be sure to not crowd the chicken, and turn a couple of times to keep from burning.

Creamed Corn

Creamed corn is one of my all-time comfort foods. When you cream corn, it creates a velvety smooth texture that is just heavenly.

12 ears corn
3 tbsp. butter
$^1\!/_2$ cup cream
1 tsp. salt
$^1\!/_2$ tsp. freshly ground black pepper
1 tsp. sugar

Shuck the corn and remove the silk. Cut the kernels from the cob and scrape all of the "corn milk" into a bowl. Melt butter in a skillet over medium heat. Add corn kernels and milk. Add remaining ingredients, mixing well. Cook for 8 minutes, or until corn is tender. Cover, remove from heat, and allow to rest for 5 minutes before serving.

Cornbread

Cornbread is a Southern dining staple, and this recipe is foolproof!

2 eggs
2 cups self-rising yellow cornmeal
2 tbsp. sugar
⅓ cup neutral oil
1⅓ cups buttermilk

Lightly beat eggs. Add remaining ingredients and mix well. Pour into a greased 8" x 8" pan and bake at 400 degrees for 20 to 25 minutes.

Cornbread Salad

This family favorite makes a beautiful presentation when layered in a glass bowl. Ribbons of color in bright red, green, and gold give it a festive look. When looking for the perfect dish to use for fresh summer tomatoes and Vidalia onions, look no further! This can be served at room temperature or chilled.

5 cups (1 recipe) cornbread, cubed
3 cups diced fresh tomatoes
1 cup chopped Vidalia onion
1 cup chopped green and yellow bell pepper
12 slices bacon, cooked crisp and crumbled
½ cup parmesan cheese
1 cup mayonnaise
¼ cup whole milk
½ cup sweet pickle relish, with juice

Layer the cornbread, tomatoes, onion, peppers, bacon, and cheese in a bowl. In a separate bowl, combine the mayonnaise, milk, and pickle relish. Pour mayonnaise mixture over the top of the cheese. Toss together just before serving, if you like.

Peanut Butter Pie

I cannot think of any duo that is more decadent than peanut butter and chocolate. This is my family's absolute favorite dessert! It is beautiful served on clear glass plates drizzled with chocolate syrup. Yum!

For the Crust:
1/4 cup sugar
1/2 cup butter, melted
1 1/2 cups crushed chocolate cookie crumbs

For the Filling:
1 cup cream cheese
1 cup creamy peanut butter
1 cup sugar
1 tbsp. butter
1 tsp. vanilla
1 cup heavy whipping cream, whipped

To form the crust, mix together all ingredients by hand and press into a pie plate. Bake at 375 degrees for 10 minutes. Allow to cool completely.

Meanwhile, blend cream cheese, peanut butter, sugar, butter, and vanilla until creamy. Fold whipped cream gently into mixture. Pour into prepared pie crust. Garnish with chopped peanut butter cups, shaved chocolate or chopped peanuts. Chill for 4 to 6 hours in the refrigerator or 1 hour in the freezer before serving so that the pie becomes firm and easy to slice.

Mint Sweet Tea

Sweet tea is a Southern staple, and everyone has their own favorite recipe. I like adding mint to mine—when the mint is flourishing in the summer, it adds a bright, sunny twist!

7 cups water, divided
1 cup sugar
1 cup fresh mint leaves, packed
2 family-size tea bags

Bring 1 cup water and sugar to a low boil, allowing sugar to dissolve. Remove mixture from the heat. Add mint leaves and cover, allowing to steep for 30 to 45 minutes. Remove mint leaves from the syrup. Boil remaining 6 cups of water; steep tea. Combine tea and mint syrup and chill. To serve, pour tea over ice and garnish with fresh mint leaves and lemon slices.

Wine Pairing

Sundays down South are a special time to spend with family, and great Southern cooks such as Lara Lyn carry on the hallowed tradition of the Sunday feast. A legendary wine such as a white Bordeaux will enhance the flavors and intoxicating aromas of these dishes. It is regal and elegant and seems to be crafted for serving at these festive affairs. Bordeaux is too often

thought of as expensive, elitist, or unapproachable, but white wines from this region are highly regarded. A surprising number are quite affordable, too. For Lara Lyn's pie, Sauternes, a great French dessert wine, will add luscious majesty to the finale.

Breakfast for Dinner

Serves 2

Shrimp Omelet
Lemon-Salted Home Fries

Many days, we don't have time in the mornings to enjoy the delicious offerings of a hearty breakfast. Take a break from tradition, and serve breakfast for dinner instead!

Shrimp Omelet

A rich, hearty dish, this is worthy to be called dinner! You will think that you are on vacation at the coast when you enjoy this shrimp-stuffed omelet.

2 tbsp. butter
4 eggs
¼ cup milk
¼ cup cream cheese, room temperature
2 tbsp. sour cream, room temperature
¼ cup chopped scallion
¼ lb. shrimp, peeled, deveined, cooked, and chopped
¼ cup mozzarella cheese
2 tbsp. parmesan cheese

Melt butter in a skillet or omelet pan over medium-low heat. Whisk the eggs and milk together; pour into pan. Mix the cream cheese and sour cream together. Cook the omelet until just set, gently spooning the cream-cheese mixture onto the surface. Add the scallions and shrimp to the omelet. Fold the omelet in half and place on a baking dish. Top the omelet with the mozzarella and parmesan cheeses and place the omelet under the broiler for a few seconds until cheese is melted.

Lemon-Salted Home Fries

Instead of plain hash browns, these home fries are the perfect complement to the shrimp omelet. Their hint of lemon really brightens the meal!

2 baking potatoes
1½ tsp. lemon zest
1½ tsp. Kosher salt
Canola oil, for frying

Wash and dry potatoes. Slice the potatoes ¼" thick width-wise. Combine the lemon zest and salt in a small bowl and set aside. Fry the potatoes in oil until golden brown. Drain on a paper towel. While the potatoes are still hot, sprinkle with the lemon salt.

Wine Pairing

Pour Biltmore Estate Méthode Champenoise Blanc de Noir Brut from North Carolina into lovely crystal flutes. This crisp, sparkling wine with a delightful light-pink hue features fruity flavors of raspberry and citrus that complement and blend with the cheeses in the omelet.

Georgia Rich Dinner

Serves 6

Sweet Onion Crab Dip
Georgia-Inspired Shrimp and Grits
Blue Cheese and Fig Cheesecake
Salted Whiskey Caramels

I named this menu Georgia Rich because many of the products used in the recipes can be found in Georgia. I like to use Georgia Olive Farm Olive Oil and Gayla's Grits from Lakeland, Georgia. The delicious cheese in the shrimp and grits is produced in Thomasville, Georgia, by Sweet Grass Dairies. The famous Vidalia Onions come from Vidalia, Georgia. All of these products have become staples in my kitchen. When you purchase grits, choose coarse-ground grits, as other grits are ground too fine to hold up in such a hearty dish. You may substitute a mild Gruyere cheese in this recipe and a mild sweet onion. Good quality olive oil is a must in any kitchen. Many specialty shops will allow you to taste oils and cheeses before you purchase, so have fun looking for something that you like! I prefer to use whiskey from Thirteenth Colony Distilleries in Americus, Georgia, for the salted whiskey caramels. If you do not have access to these products, substitute products readily available in your area to make the most flavorful and wholesome dishes.

Sweet Onion Crab Dip

This is a rich and delicious appetizer. However, it is hearty enough to serve as a main dish. I use Vidalia onions for this recipe, when they are available. Serve it alongside toast or crackers.

2 cups chopped sweet onion
$1/2$ cup chopped red pepper
$1/2$ cup chopped green pepper
2 cups grated Swiss cheese
2 cups mayonnaise
1 lb. lump crabmeat
1 tbsp. fresh lime juice
1 tsp. minced fresh dill

Mix all ingredients together. Pour into a buttered 9" x 9" baking dish. Bake at 350 degrees for 35 to 40 minutes or until lightly browned and bubbly.

Georgia-Inspired Shrimp and Grits

Shrimp and grits are a Southern classic. The variations are endless and change from state to state. My shrimp and grits are inspired by the Georgia products that I have right here in my own backyard!

4 cups chicken broth
2 tbsp. plus $\frac{1}{2}$ cup butter
$\frac{1}{2}$ tsp. pepper
1 cup coarse-ground grits
8 oz. gruyere cheese
2 tbsp. olive oil
1 large Vidalia onion, chopped
$\frac{1}{2}$ tsp. salt
1 tsp. sugar
1 lb. large shrimp, peeled and deveined
2 cloves garlic, minced
2 tbsp. chopped fresh rosemary

Bring the chicken broth, 2 tbsp. butter, and pepper to a boil. Add the grits to the broth mixture and cook, covered, over medium-low heat for 1 hour, stirring frequently. Add water as needed, $\frac{1}{4}$ of a cup at a time, to keep the grits from sticking to the pot. During the last 15 minutes, add the cheese, and stir to dissolve into the grits. Set aside. Place olive oil in a skillet over medium-low heat and add the onion, salt, and sugar. Cook for 20 minutes until caramelized; set aside. Spread the shrimp on a greased baking sheet. Melt the remaining $\frac{1}{2}$ cup butter and stir in garlic and rosemary. Pour the butter mixture over the shrimp, and roast in a 400-degree oven for 8 to 10 minutes or until cooked through. To serve, ladle the grits into 6 large serving bowls and top with equal portions of the onions. Place equal portions of the shrimp around the edges of the bowls.

Blue Cheese and Fig Cheesecake

Blue cheese and fig is a classic combination, so what could be better than to put them together in a sweet and savory cheesecake?

For the Crust:
2$\frac{1}{2}$ cups graham cracker crumbs
$\frac{2}{3}$ cup butter, melted
$\frac{1}{2}$ cup sugar

For the Filling:
1$\frac{1}{2}$ cups cream cheese, room temperature
$\frac{1}{2}$ cup blue cheese, room temperature
1$\frac{1}{4}$ cups sugar, divided
2 large eggs
1 tsp. vanilla
1 cup sour cream

For the Topping:
1 12-oz. jar fig preserves
$\frac{1}{2}$ cup toasted walnuts

To make the crust, combine the graham cracker crumbs, melted butter, and sugar. Press into the bottom and up the sides of a greased 10" springform pan.

Beat cream cheese and blue cheese until smooth. Add $\frac{3}{4}$ cup sugar; beat until smooth. Add eggs, one at a time. Add vanilla and mix well. Pour the mixture over the crust. Bake at 350 degrees for 60 to 65 minutes or at 325 degrees if you are using a dark pan. While the cake bakes, whip the sour cream and remaining $\frac{1}{2}$ cup sugar on high for 3 to 4 minutes. When the cake is done baking, remove from the oven and pour the mixture over the cake while it is still hot. Return the cake to the oven and bake for an additional 10 minutes. Once cool enough to handle, remove from pan. Cool the cake completely, then chill for 3 hours.

Before serving, top with fig preserves and toasted walnuts.

Salted Whiskey Caramels

Who says that candy is just for kids?

2 cups light brown sugar, packed
1 5-oz. can evaporated milk
$\frac{1}{2}$ cup butter
2 tbsp. whiskey
1 cup chopped, toasted pecans or walnuts
1 tbsp. kosher salt

Combine the brown sugar, evaporated milk, and butter in a heavy pot. Cook the mixture over low heat, stirring constantly until the butter melts. Raise the heat to medium-high and stir constantly until the mixture comes to a boil. Boil for 3 minutes. Remove the pot from the heat and add the whiskey. Pour the mixture into a mixing bowl and beat until the mixture cools slightly and becomes the consistency of icing. Add the nuts and mix until just blended. Pour into a buttered 8" x 8" pan and sprinkle with salt. Cover with plastic wrap and refrigerate until firm. Cut the caramels into squares.

Wine Pairing

Rob Mondavi Jr., the co-founder of the Michael Mondavi Family Estate winery, has a special Georgia connection: his wife, Lydia, is an Atlanta native. Rob's choice for Lara Lyn's spectacular shrimp and grits is his family's Isabel Mondavi Deep Rosé. This luxurious Cabernet Sauvignon is notable for its captivating aromas of strawberry, cranberry, and red apple. The mouthwatering acidity and juicy finish make this wine ideal for pairing with the tantalizing tastes on this menu.

Sunny Summer Lunch

Serves 4

Grilled Summer Vegetable Sandwich
Herb-Roasted Potato Fries
Rum Parfaits

The summer sun warms our days, and this lunch menu will warm your heart. Packed with delicious summer vegetables, this menu is the perfect celebration of fresh produce and family-filled summer memories.

Grilled Summer Vegetable Sandwich

These vegetables are tasty grilled or roasted in the oven. This recipes makes one large sandwich to cut into 4 servings.

1 eggplant, sliced ¼" thick
1 sweet onion, sliced ¼" thick
2 yellow squash, sliced ¼" thick
1 zucchini, sliced ¼" thick
Olive oil
Salt to taste
Pepper to taste
1 tsp. dried basil
1 loaf ciabatta or Italian bread
3 slices provolone cheese
Balsamic vinegar

Brush both sides of sliced vegetables with olive oil. Season with salt, pepper, and basil. Grill vegetables until tender, approximately 6 minutes on each side. While the vegetables grill, slice the bread lengthwise and brush with olive oil. Remove the vegetables from the grill. Grill the bread until lightly golden. Place the provolone cheese slices on the bread, followed by vegetables, then drizzle with olive oil and balsamic vinegar.

Herb-Roasted Potato Fries

Rosemary adds delicious flavor to a plain potato.

2 lbs. Russet potatoes, washed
¼ cup olive oil
2 tbsp. Kosher salt
1 tsp. black pepper
1 tbsp. chopped fresh rosemary
Zest of 1 large lemon

Cut each potato into 12 pieces by slicing into thirds lengthwise and then into quarters. Place fries in a bowl, and pour olive oil over them. Toss fries with hands to coat well. Arrange fries on a baking sheet lined with parchment paper, making sure they are spread evenly. In a small bowl, combine salt, pepper, rosemary, and lemon zest. Sprinkle salt mixture evenly over potatoes. Bake the potatoes at 425 degrees for 35 minutes until golden brown.

Rum Parfaits

This is a simple yet elegant dessert. Most of the components can be prepared ahead of time, so all you need to do is assemble and serve! If you prefer, substitute the raspberries for blackberries and the raspberry preserves for blackberry preserves.

2 3-oz. boxes French Vanilla instant pudding mix
3½ cups whole milk
½ cup 151-proof rum
1 cup whipped cream
Pound cake, for serving
Raspberries, for serving
Raspberry preserves, for serving

In a large mixing bowl, combine the pudding mix and milk. Slowly add the rum, mixing well. Gently fold in the whipped cream until mixture is smooth. Cover with plastic wrap. Refrigerate the mixture for 6 to 8 hours or overnight. Cut the pound cake into 1" cubes. Arrange the parfaits in a glass, layering the ingredients as follows: 3 to 4 cubes pound cake, 1 tbsp. preserves, ¼ cup rum mixture, and 4 to 5 berries. Continue layering until the top of the glass is reached.

Wine Pairing

Wisdom Oak Winery's Cabernet Franc mirrors the history and vision of the Monticello Wine Region of Virginia. This memorable delight suggests to the same flavors of a good French Burgundy. It is mysterious and enjoyable. Dreaming Tree Wines, created by Dave Matthews and award-winning winemaker Steve Reeder, has a wonderful Central Coast Chardonnay that pairs delightfully with Lara Lyn's lunch.

Light Coastal Delight

Serves 4

Roasted Red Snapper
Zesty Asparagus
Fresh Berries with Lemon-Scented
Whipped Cream

Whoever said that light and healthy can't be flavorful has definitely not tried these recipes. Everything is as fresh—and delightful—as a coastal breeze.

Roasted Red Snapper

I love fresh seafood. This fish is full of flavor without a lot of work.

4 8-oz. red snapper fillets
4 tbsp. olive oil
2 tsp. salt
1 tsp. freshly ground black pepper
1 cup sliced cherry tomatoes
$1/4$ cup sliced sweet onion
$1/2$ cup chopped fresh basil
2 lemons, divided

Arrange fish on a foil-lined baking sheet coated with non-stick cooking spray. Drizzle fish with olive oil and sprinkle with salt and pepper. Arrange tomatoes, onion, and basil, on top of the fish. Slice 1 lemon; place slices on top of basil. Bake at 400 degrees for 20 minutes. Remove fish from the oven and squeeze the juice of remaining lemon over the fillets.

Zesty Asparagus

Fresh asparagus are a bright accompaniment to the fish and a break from a simple baked potato.

1 lb. asparagus
2 tbsp. olive oil
1 tsp. coarse salt
$\frac{1}{2}$ tsp. freshly ground black pepper
2 tbsp. lemon juice
1 tbsp. Dijon mustard

Wash and dry the asparagus. Cut off the bottom $\frac{1}{2}$" of stem to remove any toughness. In a large bowl, whisk the remaining ingredients together. Add the asparagus to the bowl with oil mixture and toss well to coat. Spread the asparagus on a parchment paper-lined baking sheet. Bake at 400 degrees for 10 to 12 minutes.

Fresh Berries with Lemon-Scented Whipped Cream

Desserts don't have to be heavy to be sensational. These berries are bursting with flavor!

1 cup fresh blueberries
1 cup fresh raspberries
1 cup fresh strawberries, halved
3 tbsp. sugar, divided
1 cup heavy whipping cream
1 tbsp. lemon zest

Thoroughly wash all of the berries. Combine berries and toss with 1 tbsp. of the sugar. In a mixing bowl, whip the heavy whipping cream, lemon zest, and remaining 2 tbsp. sugar until soft peaks form. Divide the berries into four bowls and top with dollops of whipped cream.

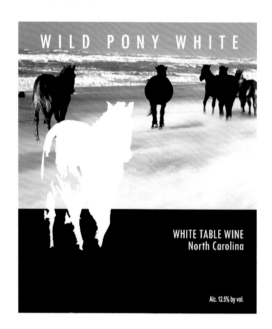

Wine Pairing

North Carolina's Currituck County in the fabled Outer Banks is home to Sanctuary Vineyards, where wonderful wines are the end result from grapes enriched by the coastal soil and Atlantic breezes. Wild Pony White blends 80 percent Chardonnay and 20 percent Riesling and offers apple, pear, and stone-fruit flavors that soar with Lara Lyn's superb fish recipe.

Weekend Fall Breakfast

Serves 6-8

Baked Grits
Mustard-Glazed Bacon
Miss Peggy's Mustard Sauce
Pumpkin Muffins
Seasoned Apples
Hot Spiced Tea

The arrival of fall makes one want to slow down and enjoy the cool weather after the hot days of summer. Starting out a morning with this breakfast will put you in the mood to take a walk outside and enjoy the changing colors of the leaves!

Baked Grits

Grits are as Southern as you can get. Breakfast, lunch, or dinner, grits are the perfect accompaniment. This baked version adds some hearty texture to a traditional offering.

2 cups water
2 cups chicken broth
1 cup grits, not instant
1 tsp. salt
3 tbsp. butter, room temperature
2 eggs, whipped

In a medium-size pot, bring water and broth to a boil. Add grits and cook until done according to package directions. Remove grits from heat and add salt, butter, and eggs. Pour into a greased 2-quart casserole dish and bake at 350 degrees for 45 minutes.

Mustard-Glazed Bacon

This is such a treat from traditional bacon! The mustard here works well on sausage, too.

1 lb. bacon
½ cup Miss Peggy's Mustard Sauce (see below)

Lay bacon on a large baking sheet and spread top side only with mustard sauce. Bake at 400 degrees for 10 minutes or until bacon is done. Monitor the bacon as it cooks; cooking time may need to be adjusted depending on the thickness of the bacon.

Miss Peggy's Mustard Sauce

Miss Peggy was my dance teacher, as she was to thousands of other girls over the sixty-plus years that she taught. Miss Peggy would always give a jar to me when she made it. The sauce originated with a friend of her mother's and even was served at Miss Peggy's wedding! Her daughter Paige gave me this recipe. It is delicious on hot dogs, sandwiches, and pork!

4 tbsp. dry mustard
1 1/2 cups white sugar
1/4 cup light brown sugar
5 1/2 tbsp. malt vinegar
24 oz. yellow mustard

Mix all ingredients together and store in the refrigerator for up to 4 weeks.

Pumpkin Muffins

When these start baking, the smell of fall arrives in your oven. Serving these with cream cheese is an extra-delicious treat.

2½ cups white sugar
½ cup brown sugar
⅓ cup canola oil
4 eggs, beaten
1 16-oz. can pumpkin
3½ cups all-purpose flour
2 tsp. salt
1 tsp. baking powder
1 tsp. nutmeg
1 tsp. cinnamon
1 tsp. allspice
½ tsp. cloves
⅔ cup water
¾ cup chopped walnuts or pecans

In a large bowl, beat together both sugars, oil, eggs, and pumpkin. In a separate bowl, combine flour, salt, baking powder, nutmeg, cinnamon, allspice, and cloves. Add dry mixture to the pumpkin mixture, alternating with water until all is incorporated. Add nuts and stir gently. Fill 18 greased or paper-lined muffin cups and bake at 350 degrees for 15 to 18 minutes until a toothpick inserted in the center comes out clean.

Seasoned Apples

This recipe allows the natural sweetness of the apples to emerge without being overpowered by sugar.

2 tbsp. olive oil
3 sweet and 3 tart apples, cored and sliced
$\frac{1}{2}$ cup brown sugar
1 tsp. cinnamon

Heat the olive oil in a skillet over medium heat. In a bowl, combine the apple slices and brown sugar together, coating the apples thoroughly with the sugar. Arrange apple slices evenly in the skillet and cook, covered, over medium heat for 4 minutes. Turn the apple slices over and sprinkle the cinnamon over the apples. Cook 4 more minutes, and turn off the heat. Allow the apples to rest, covered, for 15 minutes before serving.

Hot Spiced Tea

My mother made this on cool days. I can remember how the house filled with the smell of spices. Nothing was better than a hot cup of this tea by the fire!

4 cups water
3 family-size black tea bags
3 cinnamon sticks
8 cloves
1 cup sugar
Juice of 2 oranges
Juice of 1 lemon

In a pot, combine water, tea bags, cinnamon sticks, and cloves. Bring mixture to a boil, then remove from heat and cover. Allow tea to steep for 30 minutes. Place sugar in a pitcher. Strain tea into the pitcher and discard spices. Add orange and lemon juice and stir. Serve warm. Drink immediately or keep in a pitcher in the refrigerator for 3 to 4 days.

Football Kick-Off Party

Serves 6-8

Black Bean Salsa
Blue Cheese Wafers
Frosted Pecans
Pork Sliders with Mustard Sauce
Marinated Slaw
Potato Skewers
Pecan Brittle

When it comes to football season in the South, people automatically think of SEC Football. When it comes to football season in my house, I think of Knights Football! For a mama with a son playing for his high school football team, this means wearing our red, white, and blue. Knight's football means championship games, loud noise makers, and tailgating. Hometown high school football gets a hold of you like nothing else, and these recipes are sure to make your kick-off party a hit!

Black Bean Salsa

This is a crowd pleaser, perfect for a variety of menus.

2 15-oz. cans black beans, drained
1 16-oz. can whole kernel corn, drained
1 16-oz. can chopped tomatoes
1 10-oz. can Rotel tomatoes with peppers
½ cup chopped fresh cilantro
6 tbsp. freshly squeezed lime juice
6 tbsp. canola oil
½ cup finely chopped Vidalia onion
1½ tsp. cumin
¼ tsp. salt
¼ tsp. pepper

Mix all ingredients together in a large bowl. Let rest for 2-3 hours to allow flavors to blend. Serve with chips or as a side dish.

Blue Cheese Wafers

If you are looking for a twist on traditional cheese straws, then you will love these!

$^1/_2$ cup unsalted butter, room temperature
8 oz. blue cheese
$1^3/_4$ cups all-purpose flour
1 tsp. Worcestershire sauce
$^1/_4$ tsp. cayenne pepper
2 cups toasted rice cereal

Combine the first 5 ingredients (through cayenne pepper) in a food processor and blend until mixture is smooth. Add cereal and blend until just combined. Roll dough into small balls about the size of a walnut. Place balls on a parchment paper-lined baking sheet, and press balls flat with a fork. Bake at 325 degrees for 25 to 28 minutes.

Frosted Pecans

The combination of sugar, spice, and pecans is better than candy.

1 egg white, beaten until stiff
$^1/_2$ cup sugar
1 tsp. cinnamon
1 lb. pecan halves

Combine egg, sugar, and cinnamon, and toss with pecans. Pour coated pecans on a parchment paper-lined baking sheet and bake at 350 degrees for 20 to 25 minutes or until set.

Pork Sliders with Mustard Sauce

Who says that burgers have to be beef? These pork sliders are a hit at any cookout or tailgate.

2 lbs. ground pork
2 cloves garlic, minced
1 tbsp. fresh thyme
1 tsp. salt
$^1/_2$ tsp. pepper
Sliced Vidalia onions, for serving
Miss Peggy's Mustard Sauce, for serving

Mix pork, garlic, thyme, salt, and pepper by hand until combined. Form into 16 mini burgers. Grill over medium heat, 5 minutes per side, or until the center reaches 145 degrees. Serve sliders with sliced Vidalia onions and mustard sauce on Hawaiian rolls.

Marinated Slaw

Looking for a change from a traditional, cream-based slaw? Look no further! This is great as a side dish or as a topping for hot dogs, barbeque, and tacos!

1 cabbage, shredded
1 cup shredded carrots
1 cup apple cider vinegar
2 tbsp. olive oil
$1/2$ cup sugar
$1/2$ tsp. salt
$1/2$ tsp. dry mustard
$1/2$ tsp. celery seeds

Place cabbage and carrots in a large bowl. In a separate bowl, whisk together remaining ingredients; pour over vegetables and toss to coat. Cover, chill, and allow to marinate for 2 to 3 hours.

Potato Skewers

These are so much fun to have at a football party or event. Having them on a skewer makes them a fun finger food!

$2^1/2$ lbs. Baby Dutch Gold potatoes
$1/2$ cup honey
2 tbsp. Dijon mustard
3 tbsp. balsamic vinegar

Boil the potatoes until just tender; do not overcook. Thread potatoes onto 8 wooden skewers that have been soaked in water to prevent burning. In a small bowl, combine honey, mustard, and vinegar to make a glaze. Grill potato skewers over medium heat; baste with glaze. Cook for 6 to 8 minutes and flip over. Baste the other side and cook for another 6 to 8 minutes.

Pecan Brittle

These are a favorite for tailgating. An easy-to-hold dessert is just what you need—no plates or forks to worry about! This is easy to make and easy to eat, and everyone loves it.

1 cup sugar
½ cup light corn syrup
1 cup pecans, roughly chopped
1 tsp. butter
1 tsp. vanilla
1 tsp. baking soda

Mix sugar and corn syrup in a quart-size microwavable bowl. Microwave the sugar and syrup mixture on high for 4 minutes. Add pecans to mixture, stir, and microwave for 3 minutes. Add the butter and vanilla, stirring well. Microwave for 2 more minutes, then remove from the microwave. It should have a light caramel color. Add the baking soda and stir until foamy. Pour onto a heavily greased cookie sheet and allow it to spread on its own. *Do not spread it yourself!* When the brittle is completely cool, break it into pieces and store in airtight containers. Since all microwaves are different, you may need to adjust the times based on your microwave.

Wine Pairing

Just before toe meets leather, creative food of all sorts appears. Lara Lyn's menu satisfies the appetites of enthusiastic fans by providing simple but tasty items, all with her trademark South Georgia touch. Easy is the controlling factor here, and few wines are tastier and more flexible than a dry but full-bodied rosé. There are many pretenders on the shelves, offering sweet and pink-colored wine. While some are delicious, a blush wine is just not the same as a sun-blushed rosé from Provence. Like love, you can't beat the real thing. If there's one misconception about rosé wines, it's that they're all sweet, but sun-blushed rosés from Provence are just the opposite of blush wines. Crisp and clean, they go with everything. To get started, look for Château Montaud Côtes du Provence rosé or any similar wine from Provence.

Salute to Columbus Day Dinner

Serves 6

Italian Chicken
South Georgia Pecan Pesto Bread
Amaretto Chocolate Cake

Without Christopher Columbus, America's history could have been very different. Columbus was born in the Republic of Genoa, part of today's Italy. In honor of his impact on our country, why not put a little Southern twist on some Italian dishes? This chicken recipe came from my great-uncle, Ted Manganero. He was a full-blooded Italian from Hell's Kitchen, New York, who married my great-aunt Lillian from Valdosta, Georgia. How, you ask, did an Italian from New York end up meeting a young lady from Valdosta? Well, there was this event happening called World War II, and Ted was stationed at Moody Air Force Base. My great-aunt and uncle were a beautiful couple—they looked like a glamorous Hollywood duo! He had dark, rugged looks, and she looked like a porcelain doll.

Italian Chicken

This is a wonderful meal for any occasion and very easy to prepare. You can substitute red potatoes for the Russet, if you prefer. If you're making the substitution, increase the potato count to 12.

2 cans English sweet peas
1 cup water
6 Russet potatoes, peeled and quartered
1 large chicken, cut into pieces, or 6 breasts
1 clove garlic, minced
2 tbsp. dried oregano
2 tbsp. dried parsley
2 tsp. salt

Grease a 9" x 13" pan with olive oil. Pour peas, including the liquid, in the bottom of the baking dish; add water. Arrange the potatoes and chicken on top of peas. Sprinkle garlic, oregano, parsley, and salt over chicken and potatoes. Bake for 1¼ hours at 350 degrees.

South Georgia Pecan Pesto Bread

Yes, there is a Southern version of pesto, and besides bread, it also works well with pasta, chicken, fish, or vegetables. The possibilities are endless! The pecans and local olive oil give an amazing flavor! Feel free to make the pesto a day in advance.

2 cups fresh basil leaves, packed
1/4 cup pecans, toasted
1 clove garlic, chopped
Juice of 1 lemon
1/2 tsp. salt
1/4 tsp. freshly ground black pepper
1 cup local olive oil
1/2 cup freshly grated parmesan cheese

In a food processor, blend basil, pecans, garlic, lemon juice, salt, and pepper until finely chopped. With the food processor still running, add olive oil to obtain a smooth but still thick consistency. Transfer mixture to a bowl and blend in cheese. Split 1 large loaf of your favorite bread (such as Italian) and top with pesto. Toast under the broiler until warm and cheese is golden.

Amaretto Chocolate Cake

Some things improve with age: cheese, wine, and this cake! The flavors of the Amaretto and chocolate come together with a velvety texture. When they join together, they are far more delicious than by themselves. Making this cake a couple of days ahead of time allows the flavors to develop. Because of the alcohol, it won't go stale as a traditional cake would. It may be tempting to take a piece right away, but wait—you will be glad you did. This cake also freezes beautifully.

For the Cake:
3 oz. semi-sweet baking chocolate
$\frac{1}{2}$ cup hot water
1 cup sweet whipped butter, room temperature
2 cups sugar
$\frac{1}{2}$ cup Amaretto
4 eggs, room temperature
$2\frac{1}{4}$ cups all-purpose flour
1 tsp. baking soda
1 tsp. salt
1 cup sour cream

For the Frosting:
12 oz. semi-sweet chocolate chips
$\frac{1}{3}$ cup sweet whipped butter
$1\frac{1}{2}$ cups 4X confectioners' sugar
$\frac{1}{4}$ cup amaretto
2 eggs

To make the cake, stir chocolate into the hot water to melt; let cool slightly. In a separate bowl, beat butter, sugar, and amaretto together. Slowly beat in chocolate. Add eggs one at a time, beating well after each egg. Beat in flour, baking soda, salt, and sour cream at low speed. Bake mixture in three greased, round 8" cake pans at 350 degrees for 20 to 25 minutes or until a toothpick inserted in the center comes out clean. Cool completely.

To make the frosting, melt chocolate in a double boiler and allow to cool. In a separate bowl, beat butter, confectioners' sugar, and amaretto together. Add melted chocolate and eggs and beat until smooth.

To compose the cake, spread frosting on top of one cake layer. Place second cake on top of frosting and repeat with remaining cake. Spread remaining frosting on top and sides.

Wine Pairing

The Italian wines available today are vast, reflecting Old World regions and traditions that provide New World consumers with so many good choices. As with all wines that are becoming more available to consumers, choosing a wine that is compatible with a variety of dishes can be daunting. Light, delicate, and not overly alcoholic, Soave Classico has a place on this table, as would a refreshing Prosecco. If you prefer a red wine, look for the underrated Primitivo. This wine, loaded with mystique, can trace its lineage from the ancient Phoenicians. There even is a legend that Primitivo was served at the Last Supper. Primitivo comes from Puglia, the heel of Italy's boot, and is a very close relative of a popular American red wine Zinfandel.

Fall Is in the Air Dinner

Serves 6

Herbed Pork Loin
Twice-Baked Sweet Potatoes
Pear and Pecan Salad
Honey Cornbread Sticks
Gingerbread

There are certain foods and flavors that reflect fall. The warm spices and hearty goodness of fall's bounty come together in perfect harmony in this meal.

Herbed Pork Loin

Fresh herbs really make recipes pop. The crust that forms on this pork loin adds a layer of flavor that is fresh and delicious.

3 lb. pork tenderloin
¼ cup olive oil, divided
¼ cup plain breadcrumbs
1 clove garlic, minced
2 tsp. chopped fresh thyme
2 tsp. chopped fresh rosemary
1 tsp. lemon zest

Place pork on a lined baking sheet. Drizzle 1 tbsp. of the olive oil on pork and rub over meat. Combine the remaining ingredients and rub onto meat. Roast pork in the oven at 375 degrees for 50 to 60 minutes or until internal temperature reaches 160 degrees. Cool for 10 minutes before slicing.

Twice-Baked Sweet Potatoes

These are heavenly. They also are easy to make ahead of time and warm up right before eating.

6 sweet potatoes, washed and dried
Olive oil, enough to coat
¼ cup butter, room temperature
⅓ cup crème fraîche
2 tbsp. brown sugar
⅓ cup chopped, toasted pecans
1 tsp. ground cinnamon

Rub potatoes with olive oil. Place on a pan and roast at 400 degrees for 1 hour. Allow to cool slightly so that you can handle the potato. Cut off the top quarter of the potato and scoop out the flesh into a large bowl. Be sure that the skin does not tear. To the potato flesh, add butter, crème fraîche, brown sugar, pecans, and cinnamon, and stir well. Carefully stuff the mixture evenly back into the potato skins. Return the potatoes to a 350-degree oven for about 20 minutes to warm thoroughly.

Pear and Pecan Salad

This salad is the essence of fall flavors.

5 pears, halved and cored
1 tbsp. sherry vinegar
1 tbsp. red wine vinegar
3 tbsp. olive oil
1 tbsp. maple syrup
Arugula lettuce, for serving
$^1\!/_2$ cup toasted pecans
$^1\!/_2$ cup crumbled blue cheese

Roast pears in a 350-degree oven for 20 to 25 minutes to soften. In a small bowl, make a vinaigrette by whisking together sherry vinegar, red wine vinegar, olive oil, and maple syrup. Arrange pears on bed of arugula lettuce and drizzle with vinaigrette. Sprinkle with toasted pecans and cheese.

Honey Cornbread Sticks

The hint of sweetness that comes from the honey pairs perfectly with any meal.

2 cups self-rising yellow cornmeal
$^1/_4$ cup sugar
$^1/_2$ tsp. salt
2 eggs, lightly beaten
1 cup heavy cream
$^1/_4$ cup vegetable oil
$^1/_3$ cup honey

Mix dry ingredients together. To the dry mixture, add eggs, cream, oil, and honey, beating until well blended. Bake in a well-greased cast-iron corn stick pan at 400 degrees for 15 minutes or until golden.

Gingerbread

If you could bottle the smell of autumn, it would smell like gingerbread.

⅓ cup vegetable shortening
⅔ cup boiling water
1 egg, beaten
1 cup molasses
2¾ cups all-purpose flour
1½ tsp. baking soda
½ tsp. salt
1 tsp. ground cinnamon
1½ tsp. ground ginger
¼ tsp. ground cloves
¼ tsp. ground allspice

Melt shortening in water. Mix egg and molasses with shortening mixture. In a separate bowl, sift dry ingredients together; add to wet mixture, mixing well. Pour batter in a greased 8" x 8" cake pan and bake at 350 degrees for 30 to 35 minutes. Cool slightly and serve with whipped cream.

Wine Pairing

Autumn brings back memories of special meals. Good food enjoyed with fine wine blends well with the nostalgia of the harvest season and introduces some anticipation of upcoming holiday celebrations. Cynthiana is one of our American grapes, and wine from this delicious fruit is as different from Muscadine as night from day. The grape was known to the Cherokee as well as Thomas Jefferson. Soon after Jefferson's death, Cynthiana was cultivated in Virginia to be made into wine. Often called Norton, it compares in taste to the French Syrah and is genuinely food friendly. Stone Hill in Missouri, Three Sisters and Tiger Mountain in Georgia, and Virginia's Horton Vineyards are just a few highly regarded producers of Cynthiana/Norton. The cornerstone of Missouri's wine industry, Norton is the state's official grape.

The Hunt Supper

Serves 8-10

Grilled Dove
Sweet and Savory Quail
Vidalia Onion Casserole
Marinated Salad
Buttermilk Biscuits
Fig Preserves
Chocolate Pecan Pie

The fall in South Georgia always brings the hunting season. For as long as I can remember, we always have enjoyed dinners starring dove, venison, and quail, fried, grilled, or slow-roasted, with rich, flavorful side dishes that are my definition of "comfort food." Who better with which to share this warm and rich meal than a family of friends?

Not all of my friends are originally from the South, so I decided to invite them over for a hunt supper! I planned the menu, decorated the table in beautiful jade green- and umber-colored china and stemware. For the centerpiece, I used deer antlers, feathers, candles, and greenery. It was perfect! Surrounding my table were people from South Georgia, England, Mexico, Germany, and Nigeria— how is that for a guest list? As we enjoyed the flavor and aromas of the food and white wine, I explained the meal and answered questions regarding hunting (with the assistance of my Southern friends). Needless to say, it was a hit! The hunt supper became a tradition and is one of our favorite meals to share every year.

Grilled Dove

My Aunt Lee and Uncle Steve cooked dove like this. Many times, the dove didn't make it to the table—they were so tender and delicious that we ate them as they came right off of the grill!

12 dove breasts, cleaned
2 cups orange juice
1 tbsp. orange zest
2 tbsp. lemon pepper
6 strips bacon

Place breasts in a shallow baking dish. Combine orange juice and zest and pour over the dove. Cover the dish and let marinate in the refrigerator overnight. Remove breasts from juice and lay on a cookie sheet or tray. Sprinkle with lemon pepper. Cut bacon in half vertically and wrap each piece around a breast; secure with a toothpick. Grill slowly on low heat for about 10 minutes or until done, being careful not to overcook. Be sure to remove the toothpicks before eating.

Sweet and Savory Quail

You will not believe how rich and wonderful these quail taste! If you can't find Mayhaw jelly, plum or peach make a great substitute. The ingredients are simple—the secret in this recipe is the slow cooking.

24 quail
1 lb. butter
1 cup sherry
1/2 cup mayhaw jelly

Place quail in a cast-iron Dutch oven. In a separate dish, melt butter; mix in sherry and jelly. Pour butter mixture over quail and cover. Bake at 250 degrees for 3 hours, basting every 30 to 45 minutes.

Vidalia Onion Casserole

It is funny how something instantly can become a family favorite. The first time I made this for my husband's family, the response was "you need to make this every time we get together!" If that won't convince you to try this, what will?

6-8 Vidalia onions, peeled and sliced
$1/2$ cup butter, melted
1 cup cream of mushroom soup
$1/2$ cup cream
$3/4$ cup butter-flavored crackers, crushed
1 cup cheese crackers, crushed
1 cup grated sharp cheddar cheese
1 cup freshly grated parmesan cheese
Smoked paprika to taste

Sauté the onions in butter until tender. In a bowl, combine soup and cream. In a second bowl, combine the cracker crumbs. In a third bowl, combine the cheese. Place half the onions in a 9" x 13" casserole dish. Top the onions with half of the soup mixture, half of the cracker crumbs, and half of the cheese. Repeat the layers again and top with smoked paprika. Bake at 350 degrees for 25 to 30 minutes until gold and bubbly.

Marinated Salad

This is such a flavorful alternative to a traditional salad. The bold colors make a stunning presentation that mimics the colors of fall.

1 15-oz. can green beans, drained
1 15-oz. can wax beans, drained
1 15-oz. can red kidney beans, drained and rinsed
1 small purple onion, thinly sliced
1 small Vidalia onion, thinly sliced
1 cup diced bell pepper
$^2/_3$ cup white balsamic vinegar
$^3/_4$ cup sugar
$^1/_3$ cup canola oil
1 tbsp. freshly ground black pepper

Place beans, onions, and bell pepper in a large bowl. In a saucepan, combine balsamic vinegar and sugar, boiling until sugar dissolves. Remove vinegar mixture from heat and whisk in the canola oil. Pour the vinegar mixture over vegetables. Sprinkle with black pepper and toss. Cover and marinate salad overnight for optimum flavor.

Buttermilk Biscuits

This is the way I learned to make biscuits as a very small girl. My Mimi made this by feel, the way she did so many things. She just knew the measurements were right! Don't worry—I included some specific quantities for you, just in case.

6 heaping spoons (2½ cups) all-purpose flour
1 tsp. baking soda
1 tsp. baking powder
1 tsp. salt
1 egg size dollop (¼ cup) shortening
¾ cup buttermilk

Combine dry ingredients in a bowl. Cut shortening into dry ingredients until well blended and smooth. Make a "tunnel" or "well" in the middle of the bowl and add buttermilk. Using your hands, blend well. Form dough into a ball and place onto floured board. Roll dough out to ½" thickness and cut with a biscuit cutter or the rim of a juice glass. Press biscuits gently onto greased pan and bake at 450 degrees for 10 minutes or until golden brown.

Fig Preserves

Every summer, the beautiful leaves of our fig tree create a cocoon in the center of the yard, putting a protective barrier around the gems that hang ripening on its branches. Although the wait sometimes seems as though it will take forever, once you have the first bite of preserves, you know it was worth it.

3 qts. fresh, ripe figs
4 cups sugar
½ cup water

Clean and dry the figs. Place all ingredients in a large pot and cook slowly over low heat until mixture forms a syrupy consistency. Spoon into quart-size jars, allow preserves to cool, and refrigerate.

Chocolate Pecan Pie

How can you go wrong when you combine rich chocolate with the buttery flavor of pecans? Well, you can't! This is the best of both worlds, classic pecan pie with a hint of chocolate. Add a hot cup of coffee and you have the perfect end to an evening.

3/4 cup sugar
3/4 cup light corn syrup
3 eggs, room temperature
1 1/2 cups chopped pecans
1 tsp. vanilla
1/8 cup butter, melted
1/2 cup chocolate chips
1 refrigerated pie crust

Mix together all ingredients through chocolate chips; pour mixture into the pie crust. Bake at 325 degrees for 45 minutes or until set. Allow the pie to cool completely before slicing.

Wine Pairing

Viognier is a delightful white wine with enough body and complexity to fit with the wild fowl that is the centerpiece of Lara Lyn's supper. A French varietal, Viognier has become popular in Southern wineries and beyond. A personal favorite comes from North Carolina's RagApple Lassie Vineyards in the heart of the Yadkin Valley. Alternatively, try a Sauvignon Blanc from any number of good American producers for this dinner. Serve chilled, and remember—these are so delicious, you'll need more than one bottle!

Giving Thanks

Serves 8

Roast Turkey with Lemon and Sage
Cranberry Salad
Oyster Cornbread Dressing
Pumpkin Pie

In 1863, when the Civil War was raging, Abraham Lincoln proclaimed a national day of "Thanksgiving and Praise to our beneficent Father who dwelleth in the Heavens." To this day, it is a day to gather our family and friends and give thanks for all of our many blessings.

Roast Turkey with Lemon and Sage

The crowning glory of your Thanksgiving table should be full of flavor and tender. This recipe will give you both.

1 10-12-lb.turkey
1 recipe Sage Butter
1 onion, cut in half
1 lemon, cut in half
1 clove garlic
1 bouquet sage or 1 cup sage leaves
1 cup white wine
2 cups chicken broth

Remove all giblets from turkey and wash inside and out; pat the turkey dry. Lift the skin away from the breast of the turkey and generously rub the breast with the sage butter. Rub the outside of the turkey with the remaining butter. Fill the cavity of the turkey with the onion, lemon, garlic, and sage. In a greased roasting pan fitted with a rack, pour in the wine and broth. Place the turkey on the rack and roast at 350 degrees for 2½ hours or until juices run clear and leg is easily removed from the bird. To prevent the turkey from becoming too dark, feel free to cover with foil for the last hour of cooking. Allow the turkey to rest for 20 minutes before carving.

Sage Butter

This butter has wonderful flavor that infuses the turkey or any poultry. It is also delicious on top of vegetables! If you don't use it right away, it will keep in the refrigerator for one week.

$^1/_2$ cup unsalted butter, room temperature
$^1/_4$ cup sage, roughly chopped
1 tsp. coarse salt

Melt butter over medium heat until bubbly. Reduce heat and add sage; allow sage and butter to simmer for 3 to 4 minutes. Remove the butter from heat and stir in the salt. Allow the butter to cool slightly, remove the sage, and pour into a small bowl.

Cranberry Salad

A fresh alternative to a classic cranberry sauce, my mother-in-law makes this every year at Thanksgiving. It is always so beautiful (and delicious) with the rich colors reflecting the spirit of fall.

$1^1/_2$ cups fresh cranberries, washed and picked over
2 cups water
2 cups sugar
2 3-oz. packages strawberry gelatin
1 15-oz. can crushed pineapple, drained
1 8-oz. can mandarin oranges, drained
$^1/_2$ cup chopped, toasted pecans

In a saucepan, cook cranberries in water and sugar until they begin to pop open. Add gelatin and stir until dissolved. Add remaining ingredients to mixture; chill to set.

Oyster Cornbread Dressing

I don't think that there is a better cook in the world than my mother. She has passed so much on to me in the kitchen—and I don't mean just recipes. I have received great advice, listened to stories, and even solved life's problems in the kitchen with her.

4 cups crumbled cornbread
2 cups crumbled white bread
1 cup chopped red bell pepper
1 cup chopped green bell pepper
1 cup chopped celery
1½ cups chopped sweet onion
¼ cup butter, melted
3 extra-large eggs, lightly beaten
1½ cups chicken broth or stock
1 pt. oysters in their liquor
1 tsp. salt
½ tsp. pepper

In a large mixing bowl, combine breads, bell peppers, celery, and onion. Add butter, eggs, and chicken broth, and mix well. Add oysters, salt, and pepper. Stir everything thoroughly and pour into a greased 9" x 13" pan. Bake, uncovered, at 400 degrees for 1¼ hours. Be sure to test in the center, as some ovens cook faster than others. Dressing should be set and firm to the touch.

Pumpkin Pie

This recipe is my go-to for a Thanksgiving tradition at its best.

3 eggs, beaten
1 cup light brown sugar, packed
2 tbsp. self-rising flour
1 15 oz. can of pumpkin purée
$\frac{1}{2}$ tsp. cinnamon
$\frac{1}{2}$ tsp. freshly grated nutmeg
$\frac{1}{2}$ tsp. ginger
$\frac{1}{2}$ tsp. cloves
$\frac{1}{2}$ tsp. allspice
1 12-oz. can evaporated milk, warmed
1 9" prepared pie crust

In a large bowl, combine eggs, brown sugar, flour, pumpkin, and spices. Gradually add the warmed milk, mixing well. Pour mixture into prepared pie crust and bake at 350 degrees for 1 hour.

Wine Pairing

This is America's iconic feast, and ideally the wines should honor our great domestic products. The best advice I ever received about wine pairings for this celebration was to offer guests variety. With so many dishes to choose from, the wines should be diverse but still complement the flavors and aromas. Riesling has adapted well in our country and is produced from Washington State to Texas and New York. It is a noble wine that will enhance the turkey and the dressing. Likewise, a spicy Gewürztraminer would enhance the multitude of flavors. You should have no trouble locating American versions. Delicious red wines for Thanksgiving include Petite Sirah, the popular Cabernet Franc, or California's classic Zinfadel. Each glass of wine will symbolically salute family and friends, a prelude to the holiday season.

Warm and Cozy Chili Supper

Serves 8

Texas Chili
Jalapeño Cheddar Cornbread
Cowboy Cookies

They say that everything is bigger in Texas. Well, so is the flavor in this meal!

Texas Chili

Nothing can be better on a cold winter night than a bowl of hot chili. This is a crowd pleaser sure to warm you up! The sirloin base instead of traditional ground beef elevates the chili with extra richness.

4 lbs. sirloin, cut into bite-size pieces
Salt and pepper to taste
2 tbsp. canola oil
2 28-oz. cans crushed tomatoes
4 15½-oz. cans dark red kidney beans
1½ cups chopped green bell pepper
2 cups chopped sweet onion
½ cup light brown sugar, packed
1 tbsp. cumin
3 tbsp. chili powder
1 tbsp. dried basil
1 tbsp. lemon zest

Season meat with salt and pepper. Pour oil in a large pot and brown beef. Add all remaining ingredients and simmer for 3 to 4 hours, stirring every 30 minutes.

Jalapeño Cheddar Cornbread

Looking for a kick in your cornbread? Well, here it is!

2 eggs
2 cups self-rising yellow cornmeal

¼ cup pickled jalapeño slices, diced
⅓ cup oil
1 cup whole milk
1 cup shredded sharp cheddar cheese

Lightly beat eggs. Add remaining ingredients to the eggs and mix well. Pour into a greased 8" x 8" pan, and bake at 400 degrees for 20 to 25 minutes or until golden.

Cowboy Cookies

These are called cowboy cookies because they have a chuckwagon load of goodies in them. Thick and chunky, they are a handful! Yee-haw!

1 cup butter, room temperature
2¼ cups brown sugar, packed
⅓ cup white sugar
2 eggs, room temperature
½ tsp. vanilla extract
½ tsp. almond extract
3 cups all-purpose flour
½ tsp. baking soda
1 cup chopped pecans
¾ cup butterscotch chips
¾ cup chocolate chips

In a mixing bowl, cream the butter with the brown and white sugars until fluffy. Add the eggs one at a time, blending well after each addition. Mix in the vanilla and almond extracts. In a separate bowl, sift the flour and baking soda together. Add to the wet ingredients, mixing well. Gently stir in the pecans, butterscotch, and chocolate chips. On a piece of wax paper, form the dough into two balls and roll into logs; refrigerate for 12 hours. Slice cookies ¼" thick and place on a parchment paper-lined cookie sheet. Bake at 350 degrees for 8 to 10 minutes.

Wine Pairing

Dry Comal Creek wine will be a stranger to your table unless you live in Texas. The winery near San Antonio produces some of the most distinctive wines from the Black Spanish grape, a descendant of the grapes brought here centuries ago by Spanish monks and conquistadors. Far more than a liquid history lesson, each glass features incredible body, texture, and taste that is delicious and works wonderfully with the flavors of Texas and the Southwest, particularly Lara Lyn's original chili. This is a wine for the adventurous, but I've never met anyone who didn't love it.

Caroling Party

Serves 14-16

Tea Cakes
Mint Chocolate Brownies
Mimi's Lane Cake
Nina's Pralines
Ambrosia

These recipes are sure to make you sing.

Tea Cakes

This is a great cookie to make with the kids at Christmas. They will love decorating them with colored sugar!

1 cup butter, room temperature
1 cup sugar
1 large egg, beaten
1 tsp. almond extract
3 cups all-purpose flour
1 tsp. baking powder
½ tsp. baking soda
½ tsp. salt
½ cup whole milk
Colored sugar, for topping

Beat butter until creamy. Slowly add sugar, egg, and almond extract, beating well. In a separate bowl, sift flour, baking powder, baking soda, and salt together. Add 1 cup of the dry ingredients to the butter mixture, followed by half of the milk. Repeat the process again, and then add the last of the dry mixture. Divide dough in half and place each on a piece of waxed paper. Roll the dough into a log and chill for 2 to 3 hours. Slice cookies ¼" thick and arrange on a parchment-lined baking sheet. Sprinkle cookies with colored sugar and bake at 400 degrees for 7 to 8 minutes.

Mint Chocolate Brownies

I make these every Christmas. They are perfect for a crowd, and everyone loves the classic combination of chocolate and mint.

For the Brownies:
1 cup all-purpose flour
$^1/_2$ cup butter, room temperature
4 eggs, room temperature
1 tsp. vanilla
1 16-oz. can Hershey's chocolate syrup
1 cup sugar

For the Filling:
2 cups confectioner's sugar, sifted
$^1/_2$ cup butter, room temperature
1 tbsp. water
$^3/_4$ tsp. mint extract
3-4 drops green food coloring

For the topping:
1$^1/_2$ cups chocolate chips
9 tbsp. butter

To make the brownies, mix all ingredients together and pour into a greased 9" x 13" baking pan. Bake at 350 degrees for 30 minutes. Cool completely before adding the next layer.

To make the filling, mix all ingredients together, and spread on top of cooled brownies. Cover brownies and place in the refrigerator to chill.

To make the topping, melt chocolate chips and butter in a double boiler until completely melted; stir to combine. Cool slightly and spread over chilled brownies. Cover and return brownies to the refrigerator to chill completely before cutting.

Mimi's Lane Cake

I can't think of any cake that reminds me more of Christmas than my grandmother Mimi's Lane Cake. When my friend Caron O'Hanlon and I made it for a Sunday School party, we called my grandmother to walk us through the recipe to make sure we did it just as she did. I am still amazed that she never had to look back at the recipe. I suppose that she had made it so many times, she knew it by heart.

For the Cake:
1 cup butter, room temperature
2 cups sugar
1 tsp. vanilla
$3^1/_4$ cups all-purpose flour
$3^1/_2$ tsp. salt
1 cup whole milk, room temperature
8 egg whites, room temperature

For the Icing:
8 egg yolks, room temperature
$1^1/_4$ cups sugar
$^1/_2$ cup butter, room temperature
1 cup chopped pecans
1 cup chopped golden raisins
1 cup shredded sweetened coconut
$^1/_2$ cup red candied cherries
$^1/_2$ cup green candied cherries
$^1/_4$ tsp. salt
$^1/_3$ cup bourbon

To make the cake, cream the butter; add sugar gradually, beating until fluffy. Add vanilla to butter mixture. In a separate bowl, sift flour and salt together. Add dry ingredients to butter mixture, alternating with the milk until smooth. In a separate bowl, beat egg whites until stiff but not dry. Fold egg whites into batter and pour into 4 9" cake pans greased and lined with parchment paper. Bake at 375 degrees for 15 to 20 minutes, or until a toothpick inserted in the center comes out clean. Let stand for 5 minutes, then remove from pans and allow to cool.

To make the icing, beat egg yolks lightly and add sugar and butter. Pour mixture into a saucepan and cook over medium heat, stirring constantly for 5 minutes or until sugar dissolves and mixture thickens slightly and turns almost transparent. Remove the mixture from the heat and stir in the remaining ingredients. Let the mixture cool.

Alternate each layer of cake with a layer of icing. Once the cake is built, ice the sides and top of the cake. Allow cake to sit for 48 hours before serving.

Nina's Pralines

My husband's grandmother used to make me these every year at Christmas. One year, I hid the whole plate so that I didn't have to share!

1 3-oz. box vanilla pudding mix
1½ cups brown sugar
½ cup evaporated milk
3 tbsp. butter
2 tbsp. vanilla extract
2 cups chopped pecans

Bring pudding mix, brown sugar, evaporated milk, and butter to a boil in a large saucepan, stirring constantly for 3 minutes. Remove pan from the heat and add vanilla and pecans. Cool slightly, and drop by the spoonful onto waxed paper to cool completely.

Ambrosia

Ambrosia is an act of love. It takes time to prepare the oranges but the work is worth it! If you're enjoying this for breakfast, serve in individual parfait glasses. This is also beautiful served in a crystal footed bowl on a buffet or dessert table.

4 cups orange sections (about 12 oranges), with the juice
1 cup shredded, sweetened coconut
1 cup maraschino cherries
½ cup chopped pecans
1 tbsp. fresh lime juice

Mix all ingredients together. Serve chilled.

Gift Exchange Dinner with Family

Serves 8-10

Prime Rib
Horseradish Sauce
Merlot Sauce
Vidalia Onion Tart
Roasted Potatoes
Salad with Blue Cheese Dressing
Coconut Custard Pie

Nothing warms the heart at Christmas more than being surrounded by those we love. The gift of family tradition is one of the most precious to give. Celebrate the season with your family, and keep your family traditions alive.

Prime Rib

Don't over-think the prime rib. A great cut of beef needs little seasoning.

5-6 lb. prime rib
1 tsp. garlic powder
1 tsp. salt
$1/2$ tsp. pepper

Season beef with dry ingredients and place in a baking pan lined with foil or sprayed with non-stick cooking spray. Bake at 350 degrees for 1 hour 20 minutes, or when the internal temperature reaches 125 (for medium-rare). Allow the meat to rest for 20 minutes before cutting. Serve with Horseradish Sauce or Merlot Sauce.

Horseradish Sauce

Horseradish sauce is a classic condiment for prime rib. The addition of fresh parsley gives this sauce extra zing!

$1/2$ cup sour cream
$1/2$ cup mayonnaise
6 tbsp. prepared horseradish
1 tbsp. lemon juice
3 tbsp. chopped fresh parsley
$1/2$ tsp. salt
$1/2$ tsp. pepper

Blend all ingredients in a mixing bowl until everything is thoroughly combined. Store in the refrigerator.

Merlot Sauce

This is a wonderfully decadent sauce that adds flavor to beef of any kind. Try it over burgers, too! This recipe makes 1 pint.

2 cups good Merlot
1 cup ketchup
½ cup Worcestershire sauce
⅓ cup molasses
⅓ cup brown sugar
1 tsp. garlic powder
1 tsp. celery salt
2 tsp. dried basil
½ tsp. celery seeds
¼ tsp. cayenne pepper

Combine all ingredients in a medium saucepan and bring to a low boil. Turn heat down to medium-low and cook for 1 hour, stirring every 10 minutes. The sauce is done when it reduces to about half and thickens. Store the sauce in glass bottles or jars.

Vidalia Onion Tart

I make this tart year round. If Vidalia onions are not available, be sure to use a sweet onion instead.

¼ cup butter
4 cups sliced Vidalia onions
1 tsp. sugar
½ cup white wine
¼ cup chopped fresh parsley
2 cups smoked gruyere cheese
1 pre-baked 9" pie crust

Melt butter in a skillet; add onions and sugar and cook until tender. Remove skillet from heat and add wine, parsley, and cheese. Mix all ingredients well and pour into pie crust. Bake at 400 degrees until cheese is melted, about 10 to 12 minutes.

Roasted Potatoes

This is the way to wake up plain potatoes.

6 Russet potatoes, scrubbed and washed clean
⅓ cup olive oil
1 tsp. coarse salt
1 clove garlic, minced
1½ tsp. lemon pepper
¼ cup diced shallots

Cut potatoes into 1" cubes. Combine remaining ingredients and toss to coat potatoes. Pour potatoes onto a greased baking sheet and roast at 375 degrees for 40 to 45 minutes.

Salad with Blue Cheese Dressing

Here used in a salad, this Blue Cheese Dressing is wonderful on a baked potato. For a twist, try it in place of steak sauce! Store extra dressing in the refrigerator.

2 cups mayonnaise
1 cup sour cream
$^1/_4$ cup white wine vinegar
1 clove garlic, minced
$^1/_4$ cup chopped fresh parsley
$^1/_2$ tsp. coarse salt
6 oz. crumbled blue cheese
6 cups butter lettuce, for serving
Freshly ground black pepper, for serving

Combine ingredients through blue cheese together in a blender.

To serve, divide butter lettuce onto salad plates. Pour dressing over the lettuce and top with freshly ground black pepper.

Coconut Custard Pie

This is my idea of sweet comfort food—rich and creamy.

1 cup milk
$^1/_2$ cup half-and-half
1 cup sugar
$^3/_4$ cup shredded coconut
2 large eggs, beaten
3 tbsp. all-purpose flour
1 tbsp. butter, melted
$^1/_4$ tsp. vanilla extract
1 9" unbaked pie crust

In large bowl, mix together milk, half-and-half, sugar, coconut, eggs, flour, butter, and vanilla. Pour mixture into pie crust and bake at 350 degrees for 50 to 55 minutes until set. Cool before slicing.

Wine Pairing

A regal wine balances elegant food, and nothing harkens to royalty like a Bordeaux, perhaps the most highly regarded wine of them all. If Château Margaux isn't in the budget, look for more affordable bottles from Bordeaux—they are out there. Bordeaux price points are as varied as wines from any region; there's no need to break the bank. A good retail wine merchant will have Bordeaux with a price point in the range of $20, and many of these are approachable and resonate with the American palate. What are you waiting for? A domestic Bordeaux-style red wine is also worth the price. Many Napa wineries produce top Bordeaux-style wines, featuring blends of Cabernet Sauvignon, Merlot, Petit Verdot, Malbec, and Cabernet Franc that historically define this great wine. St. Supéry's renowned Napa Valley Estate Élu is an excellent example, and either this, a comparable Napa wine, or a top import from the Saint-Émilion region are superb choices for Lara Lyn's prime rib.

What Did Santa Bring?

Serves 8

Baked French Toast
Curried Fruit
Sausage Casserole

Christmas mornings are the most treasured memories for me. There has never been anything more precious than the look on my boys' faces as they walk into the family room and catch the first glimpse of what Santa left for them.

Until I was a mother, I never understood why Christmas morning had a schedule like it did at my childhood home. My parents did not want to miss that expression on my face—in fact, they wanted to save it forever! I had to wait to run in the family room until Daddy said he was ready. First, he would enter the room. Next, he would turn on the tree. Last and most importantly, he would turn on the video camera. We have hours and hours of footage of Christmas mornings and other gatherings, with no sound whatsoever. Daddy recorded every move I made, every smile, every "oh"! Mama always made a huge breakfast. It was full of dishes that she could prep the day before so that she could just pop it in the oven and let it cook while she helped me dress Barbie, play Twister, or have tea with my new tea set. We have sound with our home movies today, but the silent memories are just as precious.

Baked French Toast

Christmas morning is always special, and when you have a rich treat to indulge in, it is even better.

2 tbsp. unsalted butter
12 slices potato bread
6 large eggs
2 cups milk
1 cup heavy cream
¾ cup brown sugar
½ tsp. almond extract
2 tbsp. orange zest
Confectioners' sugar, for dusting

Grease the bottom and sides of a 9" x 13" baking dish with the butter. Layer the bread slices in the dish. In a bowl, whisk together the eggs, milk, cream, brown sugar, almond extract, and orange zest. Pour the egg mixture over the bread. Cover the dish with foil and refrigerate overnight. Bake, uncovered, at 350 degrees for 50 minutes. If it begins to brown too much, cover the casserole for the last 10 to 15 minutes of cooking. Dust the casserole with confectioner's sugar and serve with maple syrup.

Curried Fruit

This recipe turns canned fruit into a delicious treat that adds a special touch to any holiday breakfast.

1 15-oz. can pear halves
1 15-oz. can peach halves
1 15-oz. can pineapple chunks
1 cup maraschino cherries
1 cup margarine
¾ cup brown sugar
1 tsp. curry powder

Drain the fruit and arrange in a greased 8" x 8" baking dish. Melt margarine over low heat. Mix the brown sugar and curry into the melted margarine; pour the mixture over the fruit. Bake at 325 degrees for 1 hour.

Sausage Casserole

Not only is this delicious, it is wonderful to serve for dinner as well as breakfast. How can you go wrong with such a combination of sweet and savory?

2 lbs. mild bulk sausage
2 tart apples, chopped
1 small onion, chopped
2 tbsp. brown sugar
1 tbsp. orange zest
¹/₂ cup half-and-half
¹/₂ cups shredded gruyere cheese
1 sheet puff pastry

Crumble the sausage and brown in a skillet; drain on paper towels. In the same skillet, sauté the apples and onion with the brown sugar until just tender. In a large bowl, combine all ingredients together except for the pastry, and pour into a greased 9" x 13" casserole dish. Roll out the puff pastry and place on top of the casserole. Bake at 400 degrees for 20 to 25 minutes until pastry is golden.

Index